ADVANCE PRAISE FOR LOVING MAMA

"These are stories by real women who have decided to make an extraordinary commitment to idealistic parenting. This is a collection of stories that shows how they do it, why they do it, and why their choices are so worthwhile."

—Bee Lavender, Online Editor and Publisher, *Hip Mama Magazine*

"At last! A book that pulls together every aspect of attachment parenting combined with so many different experts who reside on the front lines in their field of conscious parenting. Hearing the importance of attachment parenting from different perspectives, and hearing it done with such heart makes *Loving Mama* an invitation parents cannot refuse. *Loving Mama* heralds the fact that conscious parenting is no longer seen as just an alternative, but rather an imperative."

—Kali Wendorf, Editor, *Byronchild Magazine*

"Truly inspirational! Full of love, compassion, understanding, imagination, maternal wisdom, and even parenting tips and original stories. Reading this extraordinary compilation of essays will help you comprehend how ordinary women become extraordinary mothers as they travel through the journey of motherhood. Through this book you will understand that listening to your maternal instincts (your inner voice) does not do any harm to a child but in fact creates self-confident, compassionate, tolerant children. Reading it will make you laugh, cry, and it will fill you up with positive and loving thoughts toward your children. I highly recommend it as a loving gift to any expecting, new or not so new mother, who is unsure about her parental skills or simply needs some reassurance as a parent."

—Frances Pflaumer, founder, president, and chief designer,
Mamámoda Sophisticated Breastfeeding Wear

"These essays are like a circle of women, lending their support to your convictions about mothering. Very worthwhile."

—Mariah Boone, Publisher/Editor, *Lone Star Ma: The Magazine of Progressive Texas Parenting and Children's Issues*

Loving Mama: Essays on Natural Parenting and Motherhood

Published by Hats Off Books®
610 East Delano Street, Suite 104, Tucson, Arizona   85705
U.S.A.
www.hatsoffbooks.com

International Standard Book Number: 1-58736-277-5
Library of Congress Control Number: 2003097781

LOVING MAMA

ESSAYS ON NATURAL PARENTING AND MOTHERHOOD

Edited by Tiffany Palisi

To my son, John Henry, who is leading me on my maternal journey. I love you with all my heart, soul, and spirit.

CONTENTS

Foreword   xv

Introduction   xvii

ATTACHMENT PARENTING

The Baby Is the Book
Jan Hunt, MSc   3

A Journey in Attachment Parenting
Stacie Levy   7

Attachment Parenting: Nourishing Mother and Child
Kerry Anne McIlvenna-Davis   11

The Paradox of Motherhood
Theresa M. Danna   17

My Personal Journey in Conscious Parenting
Kathy Morielli   19

The Drama of Bathtime and Other Major Productions
in Search of Comic Relief
Rachel Gathercole   25

Parenting with Love and Respect
Katherine Rolls-Carson   31

Gifts
Lynnea Weissman 35

Attachment Parenting, Naturally
Josie Bradley 37

Parenting from the Heart
Natalie Cresitello 41

Always Together—My Son and Me
Tiffany Palisi 43

Motherhood
Jeanine Ketch 47

Writer's Block
Abigail Dotson 51

Attachment Parenting: An Antidote for a Hectic Life
Carla Moquin 55

Connecting
Carolyn M. Klabin 59

Paving a New Way
Kathleen Lynch 65

BIRTH: BEFORE AND BEYOND

The Littlest Doula
Pamela Fellner 71

Story of Charlie's Arrival
Sally Flanagan 75

Home Birth, or How I Overcame Stage Fright
Talitha Sherman 83

Finding My Way Home
Rachel Gathercole   87

The Planned Home Birth but Unplanned, Unassisted Birth
of Saumaya Charles Schneider, April 11, 2002
Gwen Charles   93

The Value and Purpose of Labor Support
Jill Gerken Wodnick   99

Postpartum Depression and the Attached Mother
Amy Ekblad   103

Some Choices Just Make Themselves
Barbara Rivera   107

And Then There Were Three (A Letter to My Firstborn)
Abigail Dotson   111

My VBAC Odyssey
Amy Galarowicz   .   119

With A Little Help from Your Friends
Tina K. Mott   123

BREASTFEEDING IS BEST FEEDING

Breastfeeding
Abigail Dotson   131

Supporting Our Babies, Showing Our Breasts
Sarah J. Buckley   137

The Benefits of Extended Nursing that No Study Can
Quantify
Kim Collins   141

Not Born of My Body, but Nurtured at My Breasts
Janet Tilden   143

A Weaning Story: Notes from a Work in Progress
Bonnie Adams   151

Nursing through Adversity
Christi Colvin   157

No Num Nums...No Book!
Jeanne Holden   159

BABY WEARING

Oh, Baby, the Places We'll Go...In Our Sling!
Christine Jones Regan   165

True Love and the Right Accessories
Sue Landsman   171

It's a Sling Thing
Tiffany Palisi   175

THE CIRCUMCISION DECISION

Why We Chose Not to Circumcise
Jennifer E. Moore   183

For the Love of Paddy
Bridget Willey   187

Sam
Donna M. Rucinski Harrington   191

Intact and Proud
Maggie Reilly   195

One Mom's Essay on Making a Decision for Her Child
Jeanne Holden   197

An Educated Decision
Diane Oliver   201

Amber's Story
Amber Craig   205

It's a Boy!
Linda Stallings Gee   207

Taking the Whole Baby Home
Tiffany Palisi   211

CO-SLEEPING

"So, are you sleeping together?"
Sylvia Skaggs McTague   219

The Coziness of Co-sleeping
Sarah J. Buckley   225

Peace, Warmth, and Love
Maggie Reilly   231

Twilight Tango
Nancy Massotto   233

The Path to Sweet Dreams Is Not Paved with Tears
Tiffany Palisi   235

On Co-sleeping
Jennifer E. Moore   239

A Special Thank You   243

A Foreword From the Editor of Compleat Mother Magazine

On the farm we called it "mothering-up." When the maternal protective instincts took hold, we were assured that the newborn would be well cared for and protected. I have always looked for the circumstances that interfere with this process, but more importantly, for the ones that enhance it, particularly breastfeeding and a good birth. Loving Mama's collection of stories comes from ordinary women facing the extraordinary challenge of mothering-up in our modern society. They each come into their own heartfelt appreciation for their maternal gifts. It is a most incredible collection, and offers a heartwarming look at the contributions of women transitioning into the kind of mother every child wishes he or she would have.

This book is important because women must have an opportunity to benefit from the mistakes of others. We cannot possibly make them all ourselves. With so many women having only a few children, we don't have many chances to "get it right." Loving Mama serves as a guide to help us avoid the pitfalls of our culture's beliefs about birth and what it means to take care of our children. I have always cautioned women to listen to the sound of the voice that offers advice before following it; for instance, to listen to how mothers speak of their children before considering their suggestions about motherhood. The voices in Loving Mama are compassionate, resourceful, and clear.

This book will be a blessing to all stone-age babies. Stone-age babies don't know what century it is, or on which continent they are born, or anything about the cultural rituals and beliefs surrounding the beginnings of a new life. They hope their parents have the good sense to appreciate that they are born knowing everything about being babies and that they are master communicators. Because parents know only a little about being a parent, it is up to each child to teach them what they need to know. With *Loving Mama* as an inspiration, more people will have the good sense to listen first and always to their babies.

Each of the contributions would be a welcome addition to *Compleat Mother Magazine*. Readers of this collection of essays are fortunate to have an opportunity to surround themselves with resourceful, creative, and intuitive women. This book could be the catalyst for important changes in our cultural attitudes about becoming a loving mama to each and every child. I want to give copies to my daughters, to my mother, to my public library, and to everyone who is interested in making each baby's home the most nurturing and safe it can be.

This truly is a book that will make having children easier.

My best to you and yours,
Jody McLaughlin
Editor, *Compleat Mother Magazine*

INTRODUCTION

I never expected to be an attached mama. My pre-baby preparations consisted of getting ready for the birth and setting up the nursery. I had taken Bradley classes to prepare for a drug-free delivery with a wonderful instructor named Laura and decided on a local midwife named Tina. Both women helped prepare me for the many hours of labor and pushing that I was destined to endure. To learn about breastfeeding and find a support group before I needed one, I attended a local La Leche League meeting (at the urging of my mother, an LLL alumnus). I had visited a baby store to pick out a crib, bassinet, changing table, and stroller. I had also gone to the bookstore and found countless books on pregnancy, birth, and postpartum issues. I thought I was prepared.

Then, just two months prior to my son's birth, I went to a store called the Lactation Resource Center in nearby Chatham, New Jersey to get fitted for a nursing bra. The Lactation Resource Center is a one-stop shop for primiparas and nursing moms. They sell all sorts of nursing apparel, pregnancy wear, breastfeeding pillows, and informative books. They have a staff of Certified Lactation Consultants on hand for breastfeeding help, and they even make house calls to desperate moms who need a little help getting started with nursing.

As expected, I was easily fitted for a bra and was also given answers to questions I had been mulling over (and over, and over). But I was a bit surprised when lactation consultant Carol Smith suggested that I buy and read a book called *The Vital Touch* by Sharon Heller, PhD. She put it in my hands and said, "You have to read this book. It's really an amazing book." She explained that it was similar to the famous book *Touching*, by

Ashley Montague. My mother, who was with me and had read (and loved) Touching back in the seventies, said that if I'd read it she'd happily buy it for me. Although I was not particularly interested (I was very into fiction that particular month), I thought that since the lactation consultant highly recommended it, it couldn't hurt to give it a look.

That book changed everything. I read all about the importance of holding my baby. I read about women who went into the woods alone and came out with a baby they had delivered themselves. I read about how these women wore their babies all day in a makeshift sling, allowing the babies to nurse at will and ride skin-to-skin all day long. Conversely, I had been exposed to the very bad habit many Western mothers have of keeping their babies in plastic crates all day—from the car seat to the swing to the bassinet, rarely being held—and how babies really need to be close to their mamas, at their breasts and in their arms, for optimum development and growth.

All of a sudden, the beautiful cherry-wood crib that was sitting in the freshly painted, vast nursery seemed pointless, isolating even. My future baby's room seemed so far away from the one I shared with my husband. All the "necessary" baby stuff—the crib, the bassinet, the stroller—it all seemed so meaningless. And so, I went out and got a front carrier so that I'd be able to wear my baby around the house all day. I got a co-sleeper to attach to the side of our bed. I felt I'd redeemed myself and found the better path to motherhood.

But when labor hit at 6 a.m. on a cold Wednesday morning, all I could think about was myself. I babied myself all day, eating and rocking in my new glider, a gift from my parents. And I walked and walked and walked. Finally, I got to the point where my contractions were so painful that I thought I was in transition (little did I know). So my husband called our Bradley instructor and then our midwife and said, "We're going to have the baby now." And off to the hospital we went.

I can still feel the bite in the January air as I walked from my car, which we parked in the parking deck across from the hospital, to the front door. With each contraction, coming about every four minutes, I'd stop and fold in half, grab onto the back of my husband's coat, and cry. People kept offering to help by getting a wheelchair or a hospital employee. I grunted no and through tear-stained lips thanked them for their concern. I knew that walking would move labor along and believed that crunching into a wheelchair would make me feel, well, unhealthy.

I arrived in Labor and Delivery about twenty minutes later, desperately grasping my husband's arm. It seems it was a slow night at the hospital because I was quickly brought into a room where my midwife was waiting, smiling. She was excited that it was time to meet our little one; I was wishing she could labor for me. She sat with me while I labored, rubbing my back as I sat backwards on a chair and looked out the hospital window. I watched the sky darken and wondered if my baby would be born in the shadow of dusk or by moonlight. I distinctly remember telling her that the labor was painful, but not so painful that it warranted an epidural. Later, I'd eat those words.

After some unrecognizable amount of extremely painful time, I began to feel as though I would vomit. I wanted to just go home and forget the whole birthing thing. These are telltale signs of transition, so I told my midwife I thought it was time. She said she'd check me to see how far along I was and we'd go from there. Writhing in pain through every contraction and making deals with God in between, I reluctantly agreed. For those of you who haven't been checked for dilation during labor, be thankful. It is the worst pain you can imagine. It's as if you need to defecate, but someone has got his or her fist in your rectum while the…well, you get the picture. It's awful. I expected her to remove her hand and exclaim, "You're in transition," but instead I heard, "Well, you're five centimeters."

My heart dropped. This couldn't be. The pain was awful, unbearable even. My Bradley instructor had drilled into me the importance of resting between contractions. She advised against thinking about the last or coming contractions and told us to take them one at a time. I remembered, but my body completely ignored her wise words. With each contraction, I pleaded for lots of drugs. I asked for a C-section, the removal of an arm, anything to make the pain go away.

Somewhere around this time, my midwife came in to tell me my mother was on the phone. It seemed she wanted to talk to me. I remember thinking that the whole idea was crazy. Here I was in nauseating pain doing the most difficult thing I've ever done in my life and my mom wanted me to hang onto a receiver and chat. At that time, I couldn't begin to fathom the extreme worry she harbored as I, her baby, howled in a hospital room ten miles away from her. She wanted to be there to support me and, since she couldn't, she wanted an update. She didn't want to make small talk; she wanted to know I was okay. Poor Mom, she called so many times that as soon as I returned to reality, my midwife said, "Please call your mom."

Finally, my midwife conceded and offered me drugs. Actually, it was not so much my badgering as much as it was her concern that I was fighting the contractions, thus preventing them from doing their work. She suggested a mild painkiller to help me sleep before continuing to birth. She assured me that it would not be transmitted to the baby. It lulled me into a drug-induced sleep, and I hazily told the attending nurse that I loved her before passing out.

Hours later, I awoke to bold, ripping contractions. It felt as though my body was being torn in two, the uterus pulling towards my toes and my upper body resisting. I really believed that I would die. Truly. I was certain something was gravely wrong. *If not, I must be in transition,* I thought. I asked for my midwife and when she came in, she happily informed me that my Bradley classmate, Anna, had just given birth to a healthy little girl named Mira. No stitches, no drugs. Now it was my turn.

Motivated by Anna's bravery and skill, I was checked again and found I was still at five centimeters. This news was enough to dash my spirits to dust. While I knew that a laboring woman could jump from five centimeters to nine in no time, I was worn out and tired. I'd labored for over seventeen hours and I was only five centimeters. Dear Anna had been admitted to Labor and Delivery hours after I had and there she was, holding her baby.

Without rehashing the messy remaining ten hours of my labor, I somehow gave birth, vaginally and without an epidural (all was not lost), to my eight-pound, nine-ounce love baby named John Henry. He slithered out and was plopped onto my belly. I looked at him and then he was quickly whisked to the neonatal intensive care unit (NICU) in the room (he'd had meconium in his nose). While we waited the endless forty-five minutes for my placenta to deliver itself, I remember thinking that I was in no way equipped to be a mother. I kept wondering what I'd do with this poor little boy. So when I put him to my breast and he began crying because he couldn't latch on, I called an experienced nurse for help. She looked at the two of us, declared, "You can't nurse, you have flat nipples," and walked out of the room.

I was devastated. I'd watched my mother nurse my brother for over three years. How was it that I couldn't nurse? I immediately called my La Leche League leader for help. She gave me lots of information—hold the baby skin to skin, put him to my breast every X amount of minutes, relax—but nothing seemed to help. I requested from my nurse that the hospital's lactation consultant pay me a visit, but she was booked solid with moms who needed her before they went home with their new, nursing bundles of joy. So I tried to nurse and I cried. My midwife was able to get the baby latched on, but only when she was there. Without her help, I was lost.

During those two days and nights in the hospital, I was desperate for sleep. My son kept crying; he was hungry, cold, and clearly wanting to nurse. The fact that I was insecure and unsure of myself probably only made things more difficult. (It took my husband and I, working together, at least fifteen minutes to change a diaper.) Time and again, well-meaning nurses would come into my room and offer to watch my son for me while I slept. I never understood how any mother could sleep knowing that her child, especially as a newborn, was in the care of a stranger.

A nurse once said that a mother should rest as much as possible during the days after delivery, especially while in the hospital. She further stated that the only way to do that would be to put the needy, newborn baby in the nursery, citing, "You have the rest of your life to be a mother." All I can say is that the minute that child is born, so is its mother. After carrying a child in your body for nearly forty weeks, how could you not want to be glued to that child? You cannot put off motherhood by a few days. You can only put off the responsibility and caring that should accompany the awesome position that has been bestowed upon you by the sheer miracle of life. I was not about to do that with my precious child unless one of our lives depended on it, in which case, I'd do whatever was required to keep us both alive and well. My son and I slept (he, on my chest) on a cot on the floor—perhaps I was unable to nurse him all the time but I could always be his mother.

We limited our visitors to immediate family members. My mother-in-law, mom, and dad were the first to visit. My mom, God bless her soul, brought flowers and a giant box of chocolates, rich with fresh fruit fillings and creamy caramels. Everyone was in awe of John Henry. He was the first grandchild on both sides of the family. However, when my brother came, he was more grounded and full of humor. He looked at the baby and said, "Oh, he's got eleven toes." I looked down and began to count. Before I finished, he asked, "Didn't you count his fingers and toes?"

I hadn't. I just stared into his precious little face, completely in love and even more terrified. He was in my care and, so far, I felt I was failing him.

I pumped and syringe-fed my baby, while supplementing with formula. I hated every minute of it. I'd been leaking milk since my seventh month of pregnancy, but now I was unable to nurse. I couldn't accept that lot without a fight. The minute I got home from the hospital, I paged Maria, owner of the Lactation Resource Center and a Certified Lactation Consultant (CLC), whom I'd never met. Panic stricken, I told her that I couldn't get my son latched on, that I was afraid he was starving, and that I was in dire need of her services. She told me to relax and pump, to keep trying to nurse but to bottle-feed if necessary, and made an appointment to visit me the next day at my home.

When she arrived, I burst into tears. I was so relieved to get help. She was a kind, maternal woman, very professional and self-assured. She took a look at my breasts and agreed that I had flat nipples (which surprised me because when I'm cold, they pop, so I hadn't been prepared for this), but she believed I could nurse. She gave me nipple shields to use for a few weeks and left a big breast pump for me. My son, after being directed to my nipple by Maria, nursed for over twenty minutes on the left side and nearly as long on the other. She weighed him naked both before and after each nursing episode, and he'd gained ounces, a shockingly positive amount. This meant that he was getting milk...from my breasts!

Maria taught me all about relieving engorgement, avoiding mastitis, and listed foods, herbs, and vitamins I should stay away from during the first crucial months. She also gave me tons of handouts. For the first time, I started to believe that the whole nursing thing might actually happen for us.

It was a long few weeks. Nursing worked some of the time but didn't others. In the wee hours of the morning, my screaming and starving child ended up with a bottle of pumped breast milk in his mouth. I would be holding it in my hand while trying not to fall asleep. I'd actually stare at the digital clock—bad idea—to see how long we'd been up. My saving grace was something called My Breast Friend, a boppy type of pillow, flat on top and bottom, that Velcros around the breastfeeding mom's waist. I wore it twenty-four hours a day for the first six weeks, and used it for close to six months when nursing at home. My son would fall asleep at my breast and I'd leave him there, sleeping on the pillow, my breast in his mouth and my arms around him.

I never put him down. I held him while he slept and when he was awake. When I showered, my mother or my husband held him. His body never hit the bassinet to sleep— only for diaper changes. At night, he slept face down on my chest. I was so overwhelmed by the love and protection I felt for him that the mere thought of putting him down was unthinkable. I'd just stare at him and cry, thankful for the miraculous child I was holding, asleep in my arms.

Visitors who saw us told me I would spoil him, that I should put him down, and that by holding him around the clock I was doing him a "disservice." They said I needed a night out with my husband without our baby. They got me to question everything I was doing. Although I read and believed in every ounce of the information in *The Vital Touch*, I still felt that I needed to do more extensive research.

With John Henry in my arms (this was before I discovered the Maya Wrap sling), I went online in search of books on parenting. One that sounded interesting but had a bizarre name was called *Attachment Parenting* by Katie Alison Granju. After reading the blurb about it online, I ordered a copy. I knew nothing of attachment parenting or of the great Dr. William Sears, known to many as the father of attachment parenting, or Dr. Jay Gordon, the guru of a good night's sleep in the family bed.

When the book arrived in the mail, I began reading. I read while my son nursed in my arms and slept on my chest. Within days, I'd completed the book. I remember whispering to my mom over my angel's lush mop of dark brown hair, "Mom, what I'm doing has a name. It's called 'attachment parenting.' It sounds kind of clingy, right?" She looked at me funny and said, "Yeah. Can you call it something else?"

Call it what you will. I hung onto the phrase because it is accurate and actually quite welcoming. It took me a while to view being "attached" as a positive thing, mostly because our society prizes independence. To be truly independent, however, one must first be dependent.

I searched everywhere for solid facts about the positive aspects of attachment. I learned that in many societies, co-sleeping is the norm, extended breastfeeding is common, and slings and dashikis are so expected that people actually make them out of scarves and the like. I reread *The Vital Touch* and learned that Balinese babies do not touch their feet to the ground before they are six months old; in fact, they are usually only put down to be bathed and to sleep.

My son has never slept alone. He slept with me on a cot on the floor while in the maternity ward. For the next six months he slept face down on my chest (it finally got too hot in the summer—he'd slowly slide off me, covered in sweat, fall into the crook of my arm, then roll onto the bed). Since then, he's slept between my husband and me, and when he naps, I'm beside him, reading.

Knowing that most of the world's mothers were parenting their babies as I was gave me strength. I was able to ignore the criticism being whipped at me by others, and I was able to educate those who were concerned because they didn't quite understand. I was displaying a new model of motherhood to those whose generation believed that children were seen and not heard, and only loved when they were sleeping.

Don't get me wrong. I still had (and have) my share of discussions with people who think "Ferberizing" and other sleep-training methods are the way to go. I am approached by mothers who warn me that my son might get too attached, to which I reply, "Exactly how attached is too attached?" The best, though, are from people who seriously ask, when hearing that I rarely leave my son—and when I do, it's for a maximum of twenty minutes—"How will you handle kindergarten?" My son is two.

The whole subject of breastfeeding was, and still is, rarely broached in mixed company. It's funny that people think breastfeeding is a sexual subject because it has the word "breast" in it. When I first had my son, everyone tried to get me to put him on a feeding schedule. Even a well-respected pediatrician told me that he was "gaining too much weight" (he was fourteen pounds at six weeks) and that I should "skip night feedings." I told her I was feeding him "on demand" (should have said "on cue"), and she told me that if I always responded appropriately to his cries he'd quickly learn to manipulate me. Needless to say, I ignored her and found myself a new pediatrician. People couldn't understand why I breastfed in public, and asked to please pump and bottle-feed instead. When I didn't, they'd look away with pink cheeks and find any reason they could to disappear. Now, when my son asserts, "Mama, I wanna *nuss!*" the strangers who catch what he's saying usually drop their jaws. Once, though, a woman heard and said, "Oh, when my son was little, I nursed him, too. Isn't it great?"

I rarely need to discuss the fact that my son is intact, however, as that fact would only be known to people who watch me change his diaper. The exception is family and friends, all of whom know me so well that, if they ask any questions regarding circumcision, they know that they should get some water and take a seat because they'll be listening a long, long time. (I've written more on this subject in "Taking the Whole Baby Home" in this book.)

When my son was about a year old, my friend Kathy and I began discussing the possibility of opening a drop-in center for mothers, all mothers, to offer support and friendship as they entered motherhood. We'd answer questions, offer connections, and have an extensive lending library with back issues of *Mothering* magazine, *Welcome Home, Compleat Mother,* and other child-friendly volumes. We'd be sure to keep out books that supported cry-it-out tactics, baby training, and physical and emotional abuse. Clearly, for two mothers with toddlers and no money, this was a pipe dream. But it did evolve into a quarterly newsletter called *The Wise Mom.* Written by mothers, for mothers, this newsletter gave a voice to our local North Jersey group of conscious mothers. Moms wrote about everything from breastfeeding to co-sleeping, choices in vaccinations and circumcision, cloth diapers, soft-sole shoes, and slings.

Since then, we've put out eight issues (as of August 2003) and they have gotten more and more wonderful. I still read back issues to remind myself what a great group of mothers surround and support me with their spirit and trust in Mother Nature.

All these great essays got me thinking. What if I contacted some of the women who've written for *The Wise Mom,* and other "awake" moms (like La Leche League leaders), and asked them to write essays for a book? I decided I could sell it through attachment parenting-friendly catalogs and specialty stores so that moms who live across the country, or who feel isolated in their conscious-parenting choices, would see that they are in good company. Sometimes the road less traveled is the high road, and I believe that the mothers who have contributed to this volume have chosen it.

You will read their stories in their words. Some are professional writers and poets, some are PhDs, and many are stay-at-home moms. All tell their stories in ways that will touch your heart and profoundly change your mothering experience for the better. I have chosen not to edit the content of these stories. I believe that it is crucial to leave their final essays the way they sent them to me. They are their own creations, wonderful and whole and representative of who these women are and how they have experienced conscious parenting.

I hope that you enjoy the essays in this book. I welcome your comments and questions at thewisemom@hotmail.com or by mail at The Wise Mom, PO Box 606, Boonton, NJ 07005.

ATTACHMENT PARENTING

THE BABY IS THE BOOK

Jan Hunt, MSc

On a recent Internet radio show, I emphasized that babies are the true experts on parenting.[1] I added that I often ask new parents if they wish they had an expert living with them to help them to figure out what to do next. I told the radio audience to "Just look to the baby. If you're doing something wrong, the baby will tell you. If you're doing something right, the baby will tell you that, too. Babies know exactly what they need."

The interviewer neatly summed up these thoughts by adding, "People say the baby doesn't come with a book, but they do...the baby is the book!" Exactly. It is the baby—and only the baby—who knows just what she needs. She will give us immediate feedback on everything we do. A baby will tell us with frowns and tears when a legitimate need is not being met, and with bright smiles and cuddles when we meet her needs in a loving way. If parents can recognize and embrace this concept, parenting can be much simpler and more joyful than when the baby's communications are mistrusted and questioned.

Babies, programmed by nature, know instinctively what good parenting looks like. They know, for example, that touch is a need every bit as critical as feeding. They will protest loudly if we put them in the isolation of a crib to sleep, but will fall asleep peacefully when they have the security of human touch. They know that responsive parenting enhances trust and bonding—and they will respond with anguish and fear when we ignore their cries. They know that breastfeeding offers critical immu-

---

1. Leslie Malicote, interview by Leslie Malicote, Perfect Pregnancy and Beyond, www.wsradio.ws, 27 June 2002.

nization, nutrition, and comfort, and will instinctively move to the breast on their own, just moments after birth. They know that breast milk changes in consistency in accordance with their age, and will wean naturally when their nursing needs are no longer fully met. They know they are dependent on others for their very survival, and will react with terror if they cannot see us for even a short time. They know all of these things and more. Parents would be wise to learn from their babies instead of assuming that babies are always learning from them.[2]

Babies know many important things. What they can't know is that parents often receive harmful advice to ignore their babies' communications and to disregard their critical needs. This is a dangerous experiment, and every newspaper we read describes the long-term results of not giving children a compassionate start in life.

A baby needs what she needs, and if we meet those needs, she will thrive. This isn't "spoiling"—it is trusting that the baby is giving us important information about her legitimate needs, as well as trusting our own natural instincts to want to respond to those needs. Trusting our baby and trusting ourselves, we establish a close bond and give our baby her best chance for a healthy and happy life.

The solution is so simple and right in front of our eyes. Instead of trying to teach babies to accept parenting behaviors that are alien to their very nature, we need only allow them to teach us how to respond to their honest communication. They have so much to tell us, and they are the world's most diligent and energetic teachers.

The baby is the book. Read it—you won't be able to put it down!

Jan Hunt, MSc is the founder and director of The Natural Child Project at www.naturalchild.org, and the author of The Natural Child: Parenting from the Heart (New Society, 2001) and A Gift for Baby (forthcoming, 2003). She is a contributor to Mothering, Life Learning, Byronchild,

---

2. Jan and Tracy Kirschner, The Little Goo-roo: Lessons from Your Baby. Boulder (Colorado: Atlas Press, 1997).

and many other publications. Her *Parenting From The Heart* telephone counseling service is available worldwide for questions and concerns about attachment parenting, homeschooling, and personal matters. Jan can be reached at jan@naturalchild.org and at 866-593-1547.

A JOURNEY IN ATTACHMENT PARENTING

Stacie Levy

I did not come from what you might call an "attachment parenting" home. My mother and all of her friends and acquaintances practiced the "give it to the nanny and march it out for company" school of parenting. Children were to be seen and not heard. I thought that was all there was.

I started babysitting when I was ten. In almost every instance, the children were in a room, preferably as far from the parents as possible. The younger the child, the farther the proximity from the parent. I remember a particular little baby called Molly. She was about six months and I was about twelve. The mother left me with instructions to give her a bottle and put her in her crib and just leave her even if she cried! I may have only been twelve, but there was no way I was just going to let that poor little thing cry. So I brought her to the couch with me, lay her on my chest, and she and I went for a little snooze. No one was the wiser, except maybe for the little one who probably felt right and safe, and so could drift off easily.

When I was eighteen, I babysat for someone who would change my life. The little girl was six months old, and I was her first babysitter. How odd, I thought. Six months old and I was the first sitter! Her mother nearly cried when she had to leave her baby, and I thought, Gee, she really loves that baby! Then to top it all off, she nursed; I had never seen that before. The more I had the honor of spending time with this pair, the more in awe of the relationship I became. This was the first time I had seen a mother and baby so in love with each other. And I had seen quite a lot of mothers and babies by then. So it was no surprise that I decided that I, too, would nurse my baby and follow the example that this woman gave me.

Fifteen years later, I was pregnant with my daughter and told the doctor to write "Drugs!" really big on my chart. But then, I met yet another woman who would influence my life. She very nonchalantly lent me a copy of *Mothering* magazine, and I was hooked. I sent away for every back issue I could get my hands on. As I had not yet delivered, I had time to read them, and I am very glad that I did.

At thirty-seven weeks, I went for the hospital tour. On most of my visits to the OB, I had heard about the LDR room (Labor, Delivery, and Recovery) and how amazing it was. When we finally got to this supposedly fabulous room, the nurse seemed pleased with herself. "And here is the LDR room!" she said with a flourish. "Hopefully, it won't be too crowded when you deliver, and then you can use it."

I had been expecting soft lights and a bed that looked like a bed, but this was an operating room. What were they thinking? I burst into tears and fled the hospital, never to return. And so it was that I decided on home birth. What had seemed so outlandish at first suddenly seemed just right. So, my happy Sydnie and I began our journey, never separated for even an instant.

As she neared two years old, I started hearing, "Where are you going to send her for preschool?" All I could think of was an episode of *I Love Lucy* where big Ricky wants little Ricky to go to preschool and Lucy hides with him in the playground every day. I wasn't ready to hand her over to anyone yet. I felt as though I would be throwing her to the wolves, and so I decided to teach her myself at home.

Three years after Sydnie was born, Julian came along and was also delivered at home. At this point I have grown accustomed to all the comments I get, like, "You gave birth at home! You must be so brave!" To which I usually respond, "No you're the brave one! You went to the hospital!" And of course, "You homeschool? I don't know how you can do it. I can't wait until my kids get on that bus!"

I'd love to say that every moment of our lives is the ultimate in family bliss, but unfortunately that just wouldn't be true.

However, it only takes one Hallmark moment, like Sydnie reading to Julian as the two of them are wrapped up in a blanket on the swing, to think that all is right with the world.

Stacie Levy *was born in 1962 in New York City. She is now living in Maplewood, New Jersey with her husband and two children, and has had a lot fun getting there!*

Attachment Parenting
Nourishing Mother and Child
Kerry Anne McIlvenna-Davis

I knew absolutely nothing about attachment parenting when I gave birth to my first baby over thirteen years ago. I was eighteen years old when my beautiful daughter Alexandria was born, and although I had intended to breastfeed, difficulties with latch-on due to slightly inverted nipples, as well as a mother-in-law who told me I was starving my baby, caused me to give in to the bottles of formula the hospital had sent home with me. I dutifully obeyed my mother-in-law when she told me to never, under any circumstances, bring my baby into bed with me for fear of never getting her out. I had a "perfect" baby who slept through the night by six weeks of age, until she turned five months old and suddenly began waking five or six times every night, needing her pacifier to get back to sleep. Out of sheer desperation I put her crib next to our bed (with the side railing down) so I could just reach over to her whenever she stirred. An attachment-parenting mama was born!

I had a friend who gave me a copy of *Mothering* magazine, opening my eyes to a whole new way of connecting with my precious daughter. I began carrying her with me everywhere I would go in a Sara's Ride hip carrier, and I never left her with anyone. I began washing my own cloth diapers and making homemade baby food. She slept next to me until the age of five, when she happily moved into her new bunk bed.

One thing that I always regretted was not having breastfed Alexandria, and when I became pregnant with my second child, I began attending La Leche League meetings during my first trimester. I also bought a sling and practiced using it with dolls.

11

I received prenatal care with midwives and had a completely unmedicated birth. When I pushed Chloe Autumn into this world, my birth assistant had the wisdom to have me reach down and pull Chloe onto my chest, so only my own hands ever touched her. I immediately put her to my breast, and she latched on like a pro! I was ecstatic! I had determined that I would do everything "right" this time: breastfeeding, co-sleeping, baby wearing, cloth diapering from birth, and always following my baby's cues.

I still did not know that there was a term for my strong parenting values this time around...attachment parenting! I knew only that everything I was learning about mothering through La Leche League, *Mothering* magazine, and books like *The Continuum Concept* resonated deeply within me and caused the incredible love I had for my children to manifest itself so much more easily and purely.

I was raised in a completely nonattached manner, so being able to connect with my children so intimately also helped heal my lack of feeling loved as a child. I had divorced my husband during my second pregnancy, and was amazed by how much easier it was to be able to parent the way I wanted to, without negative influences.

Chloe was born at 11:19 p.m., on September 18, 1992, and by noon the next day, I was home. I wanted desperately to be back with Alexandria (who had never slept away from me before), and to avoid interferences from the hospital staff. I was amazed and delighted by how easy nursing Chloe was, and I held her in the sling for about ten hours a day. I only put her down to change her diaper and to have her sleep on my chest at night— she was the world's happiest baby! I was able to spend lots of time with Alexandria playing, reading, going on outings, etc., all with Chloe happily nursing in the sling. I wanted to have Chloe never know the feel of a paper diaper, so I lugged smelly cloth diapers to the Laundromat (with two kids in tow) every three nights for two years.

Chloe's main source of comfort and nourishment was always at the breast, so it was no surprise that nursing lasted for over four years. As a single mom, I had to find ways of supporting myself and my two daughters, but I couldn't stand to be away from them. So I offered childcare at home until Alexandria started school when she was five and a half, and then did something I had grappled long and hard with; I put Chloe, at the age of three, in childcare at the center attached to the local college I began attending. The experience was very difficult for me, but Chloe adjusted much more quickly than I did. The best part was being able to nurse her in the corner of her preschool before I went to classes every morning, and come see her in between classes with "milky" if she needed it.

I somehow graduated with my bachelor's in psychology three and a half years later, having had an average of four hours of sleep a night during all my college years. Being a single parent to two daughters while focusing on all of their needs and also attending college was at times extremely challenging, of course, but attachment parenting truly helped me survive. Breastfeeding was a godsend for those times I had to bring a bouncy three-year-old to class with me and needed her to stay quiet, as well as for getting her to sleep (and back to sleep) while writing a term paper. I felt like I was able to meet their needs effectively and intimately while also doing what I had to do for our long-term well-being as a family. The bonds that attachment parenting fosters is the sweetest reward for the effort we put into it.

Chloe finally weaned painlessly at the age of four years and three months (with a bit of coaxing on my part), and despite what all of the many critics told me about the damage I was doing to her, she is today a beautiful, insanely healthy and sweet eleven-year-old with no ill side effects. Extended breastfeeding in our culture is relatively rare, although the trend is picking up nowadays. It's hard to believe that something so natural and so sweet can cause so many people to become raving lunatics! People offered the most outrageous comments to me when they found out I was nursing a four-year-old (or a three-year-old, or two-year-old...) and I had a hard time dealing with it. Therefore, it is wonderful for me to be able to show those same people how fabulously well-adjusted she is and how close we are.

I remarried a little over four years ago to a man with two children of his own. On May 2, 2000, I gave birth to my third

child, so we are now a family of seven. My last birth was a culmination of everything I wanted it to be; I gave birth to my son,
Dylan, at home on our bed in the presence of an angelic midwife
who also helped me to reach down at the moment of birth and
pull my son onto my chest, literally birthing him into my own
hands. Although it was the most intense of my three births, and
more than a little painful due to back labor, it was certainly the
most fulfilling and satisfying, knowing that I did everything as
close to perfect for my son as possible. I didn't leave my bed for
several days after his birth because I had torn a little and chose
not to have stitches, and those were the happiest, most peaceful
days of my life. I stayed in bed with my newborn son, skin-to-
skin, cuddling, nursing, and resting, in a quiet room filled with
the beautiful smell of lavender oil bubbling on a candlelit dif-
fuser. (Three years later when I smell lavender, I am immediately transported to those heavenly days). I did not leave my house
until my son was ten days old, in order to make his transition
into this world as gentle as possible. I knew that I would never
have this precious newborn period back again, and so I savored
each day.

I chose not to circumcise my son, and luckily, my husband,
who is circumcised, agreed to this. I could never understand the
rationale some people gave for circumcising—that a male child
needs to look like his father. How many sons and dads sit around
comparing their penises that closely? And since a boy's penis is
inevitably going to look different from his father's for many
years, due to size difference and lack of pubic hair, how convinc-
ing is this argument? I feel that if my son wants to be circumcised
someday, he certainly can with my blessing, but it emphatically
must be his choice. I have no more a right to have his foreskin
cut off than I have to get my daughters' genitals mutilated.

✳ ✳ ✳ ✳ ✳

My son is now a beautiful, healthy, sweet, and very attached
three-year-old who nurses a few times every day and sleeps cuddled against me every night. I have held him in the sling every
day of his life, and he still likes it for short periods of time,

although at thirty-six pounds I can't do it for much longer than that, anyway. Baby wearing is one of the nicest parts of mamahood, and I believe it is as critical to infant (and child!) bonding and well-being as breastfeeding, so I made sure to hold Dylan in the sling for many, many hours every day in his first year of life, and never owned a stroller, swing, baby seat, or any other carrying/holding device for either Chloe or Dylan. And contrary to what everyone predicted, they both walked by twelve months.

It made me realize that parenting really is about ignoring those voices of "authority" (as difficult as that sometimes may be) and listening to your child as well as your own intuition. I attribute my positive growth as a human being and a mother almost entirely to following the ideals of attachment parenting. Nothing is more important to me than my children, and they are only with me for a short time before they fly off on their own. I want to hold them as close as possible now because never again will they need me this much or will I be as intimately connected to any human being. In spite of the day-to-day trials and tribulations (of which there are many in my household!) that are to be expected in life with young children, I feel so blessed to be their mother and to be allowed to shape the lives of these beautiful beings. They are my will to live, my grounding force, my joy and my treasure, and I want to be able to look back on their childhoods with as few regrets as possible.

I am so grateful that I found out about attachment parenting when I did, because it truly changed the course of my life and gave my children the secure foundation they might have missed if I had continued to parent in the mainstream way, which encourages mother/baby separation and premature "independence." The ideals embedded in the concepts of attachment parenting have fed me as a mother in some ways as much as they have fed my children, by nurturing them so thoroughly and developing these unbreakable bonds. I have been nourished myself in a hundred ways.

Kerry Anne McIlvenna-Davis *is a La Leche League Leader in San Francisco, California; the grateful mother of Alexandria, age thirteen, Chloe, age eleven, and Dylan, an intact and still-nursing three-and-a-half-year-old; and stepmother to*

Jillian, age nineteen, and Ryan, age eleven. She leads baby-wearing workshops and is a baby-sling distributor, and has been a proud member of the San Francisco chapter of Attachment Parenting International for over three years. Kerry is also an avid collector of anything Bob Dylan!

THE PARADOX OF MOTHERHOOD

Theresa M. Danna

One of the most difficult aspects of motherhood for me, especially as someone who practices attachment parenting, is that from
the moment we go into labor, our children naturally move away
from us.

It starts with the uncontrollable contractions that literally
push our baby out of our own body and into the world. Within
just a few months, our infants roll over and get their first taste of
freedom. The rolling turns into crawling, which turns into walking and running, and we end up seeing the back of their body
more than the front as we chase after them all day long. Only fear
returns them to us momentarily, and then it is like having a thir-
ty-pound barbell clamped to our legs.

All too soon, our little ones assert their independence and
individuality, from refusing to hold our hand while crossing the
street to protesting that they are "too big for hugs and kisses."
The first day of school arrives, and it is we, the mothers, who
suffer from separation anxiety.

How could Mother Nature do this to us? She gives us an
intense drive to hold and protect our children while simultaneously giving them an equally intense drive to separate from us.
How can we balance our emotions between these opposing
forces?

To help find a solution to this challenge, I turned to several
sources. One was Flow, by Mihaly Csikszentmihalyi. In his study
of creative people, he found that they innately embodied para-
doxical personality traits, such as introversion and extroversion,
responsibility and irresponsibility, rebelliousness and conserva-
tiveness, humility and pride. He believes that it is from the

17

tension of opposites that creativity emerges. Similarly, psychologist Marion Woodman, in her work with addiction, says that when we hold the tension of the opposites, our true spiritual selves come forth. And in the ancient philosophy of Taoism, it is said that the Tao—the essential life force—flows when we balance our emotions and actions between extremes. In *The Tao of Motherhood* (the most useful parenting book that I have found), Vimala McClure expresses in verse seventy-eight—"Paradox":

> A mother's nature is paradox.
> Your strength is in gentleness.
> Your authority is in receptivity.
> Your power is in letting go.

These theories all rang true for me, but I still did not know how to manage the paradox of motherhood. I would not figure out how to hold the tension until the day when I took my son to a playground that had a balance beam. While I was walking on the wooden beam, struggling to not fall, tensing leg and foot muscles in unfamiliar ways, I realized that the trick to staying balanced is to use the tension, rather than trying to eliminate it. You have to acknowledge it, get to know it, understand it, and befriend it. You have to let it work through you without questioning it. If you doubt it, you lose your balance and have to start again. Trust it, and you achieve extraordinary feats. Dance with it, and you can even spin a cartwheel along the way!

Theresa M. Danna lives in Hollywood, California with her son, AJ (born in 1998). She has a master's degree in professional writing/nonfiction from the University of Southern California and a bachelor's degree in communications/journalism from Rowan University in Glassboro, New Jersey. She and AJ can be reached at theresadanna@prodigy.net.

MY PERSONAL JOURNEY IN CONSCIOUS PARENTING

Kathy Morielli

After a long and demanding career in the computer industry in New York City, I had my son (now eight) when I was thirty-eight years old. I was mentally and emotionally unprepared to be a mother: until I birthed my son, I had never changed a diaper in my entire life. As I was getting ready to take him home from the hospital, I frantically found a nurse and asked her to show me how to put a diaper on. I watched, and practiced, and said, "Okay I can do this!" And off we went, a new family: my husband, myself, my son. My husband and I had decided that we would forgo the material advantages of two salaries, and that the best thing for our son would be to have the benefits of a stay-at-home mom. So I sequenced out of full-time corporate work into full-time mothering.

An unlikely candidate for conscious parenting, I actually had an image in my mind that I could go to the convenience store to get eggs and milk while my baby napped deeply, soundly, and safely for three hours! Given my level of information about infants, I was fortunate that breastfeeding came easily for us. I also had my older sister as a long-distance conscious-parenting model—she had breastfed and practiced co-sleeping fifteen years earlier with her daughter. I could call her for moral support—but she lived in Miami, Florida, while I resided in New Jersey. I joined La Leche League for companionship and support. I saw toddlers nursing for the first time in my life at La Leche League meetings. I thought, "Yuk! I will never do that!"

My son had other plans.

I expected that he would sleep easily and soundly in the pretty crib that my husband had hand-painted for him, in his beautifully decorated nursery. Being a normal human baby with touch and attachment needs, however, he thought otherwise. Boy, was I surprised when he did not just lie down in a lonely crib and sleep by himself. Instead, he flailed his arms, looked frantically around, and screamed! Not what I expected. I found that everyone in America had advice for me, the new mother. If I had chosen full-time daycare for my son, that would have been socially acceptable. But somehow, choosing to pick my baby up when he cried and nurse him "on demand," and even more outrageous, choosing to sleep with him, was just not considered acceptable parenting. I was some sort of neurotic mom, holding him back from developing his full personhood. On one level, the dominant American culture was ready with many baby experts (not evidence-based) who informed me to let my baby cry by himself for psychosocial reasons.

On another level, people personally gave me all sorts of conflicting advice: let the baby cry so that he could learn to develop a life of his own; he needed to be independent! So that I could go out and eat an expensive dinner without him! And I had to do establish this pattern when he was six weeks old—or else it would never happen. People also right-out told me how disgusting they thought breastfeeding was. I had a hard time coping with this barrage of "helpful" anecdotes and information. I also had strangers on the street inform me that my baby should be happy to let anyone hold him (now that would be some evolutionary adaptive twist: a basically helpless person who doesn't mind in the least if his most trusted person hands him over to a total stranger).

The information in the books from the La Leche League library held different messages: messages about basic human needs for touch, security, and attachment; and the developing brain's need for the composition of human milk. These messages made a lot of sense, and they were frequently evidence-based, meaning there was solid research referenced by the authors. In La Leche League, I actually met women who had formed a subculture and were practicing these conscious-parenting techniques together.

As I morphed from a New York City computer manager to a suburban full-time mom, I experienced a depth of love for my son that I never dreamed possible, as well as profound joy and companionship. I also experienced loneliness, isolation, insecurity, and yes, depression.

Life slowed down to a manageable pace. I got the opportunity to observe the minutiae of life: the warmth of the sun coming up, the full moon shining in my son's eyes, the butterflies feeding on the butterfly bush, seeds sprouting in the garden, my breasts interestingly filling with milk, and my baby feeding easily anywhere. He didn't cry very much at all. He was happy, smiling, as long as he was close to me. Carrying him seemed perfectly normal to me. I used a sling and a backpack, and he was so happy to be jostled about, feeling the movement of my body.

I was so afraid to co-sleep. More specifically, I was so afraid to tell anyone that I was "doing it." Like it was a dirty secret that everyone would judge. But secretly we practiced co-sleeping. And continue to do so—what a confession! And, yes, he manages to go to school and do his homework himself! Co-sleeping feels like a natural human activity to me. Ninety-five percent of the world's cultures practice co-sleeping. Of course, in America, there is a barrage of (male) experts to challenge this perfectly normal, ancient, human activity as unsafe. And also in America there is the counter in this discourse: evidence-based research that demonstrates co-sleeping to be safe.

I feel fortunate to be able to choose and practice woman-and-child-centered methods (as opposed to institution-centered methods) in my personal life. As the years pass, I notice that the movement for conscious parenting has influenced everyday practices and research. In order to remain competitive, hospitals now offer birthing suites. Women now have an array of childbirth education choices, which every year become more and more women-and-baby-centered. I am gratified to see this change, however incrementally slow, spreading throughout our society.

The American Academy of Pediatrics (AAP) and the World Health Organization recommend that breastfeeding should continue for one to two years, respectively. Formula companies are required by legislation to let moms know that breastfeeding is healthier than formula feeding. The AAP has also come out and declared that circumcision is not medically necessary. The Coalition for Improving Maternity Services (CIMS) was founded in 1996. CIMS developed a list of guidelines of mother-and-baby-centered practices. A hospital can only be designated as "mother friendly" if it adheres to these guidelines. None of these situations existed ten years ago. The collective consciousness has manifested change in our society.

I am grateful that my personal journey as a mom birthed both my professional journey as a childbirth educator and my studies in professional mental health counseling. As a practitioner of hypnosis in childbirth, I am honored by my work in assisting women with empowering methods to manage their birth experiences. In my studies of perinatal and prenatal psychology, I see that the research literature abundantly supports conscious parenting and mother- and baby-centered practices. I am grateful to have journeyed on this path with my family. I continue to be honored by the company of women along the way.

My journey as a mother was, and still is, a path of love and painful growth. I am confronted with challenges to my personal choices, and yet my parenting practices seem so normal to me. When my son was a baby, I felt him sleeping so soundly beside me; and breastfeeding was so easy. Feedings were not a long activity where I needed to get up and go into another room. We were bathed in the love and in the comfort of each other. I remember him smiling up at me one night as I cuddled him close to warm him up, as the spring night had turned a bit chilly. I felt content in that moment. And there are so many other moments to feel content in conscious parenting, and still so many to come!

Kathy Morielli is certified in HypnoBirthing, shiatsu, and Jin Shin Do, and is the author of BirthTouch: Shiatsu & Acupressure for Expectant Couples. She is a candidate for a master's in counseling psychology from Capella University. Kathy has a private practice in birth hypnosis and acupressure in Kinnelon, New Jersey, where she works with expectant families privately and in groups, and also *trains teachers in BirthTouch shiatsu and acupressure. Visit her at www.gen-tlebirthingmethods.com.*

References

Bowlby, J. 1969. *Attachment*. New York, London: Harper Collins Publishers, Inc.

Cordozo, A. 1996. *Sequencing*. Boston: Brownstone Books, Inc.

Dychtwald, K. 1977. *Bodymind*. New York: Jove Publications, Inc.

Gaskin, I. 1990. *Spiritual midwifery*. Summertown, TN: The Book Publishing Company.

Gendlin, E. 1979. *Focusing*. Tokyo, New York: Japan Publications, Inc.

Goer, H. 1999. *The thinking woman's guide to a better birth*. New York: The Berkley Publishing Group.

Hannaford, C. 1995. *Smart moves: Why learning is not all in your head*. Arlington, VA: Great Ocean Publishers.

Schore, A. 1994. *Affect regulation and the origins of the self*. Hillsdale, NJ: Lawrence Erlnaum Associates.

Sears, W. 1999. *Night-time parenting*. Chicago: La Leche League International.

Thevenin, T. 1987. *The family bed*. New York: Penguin Books.

THE DRAMA OF BATHTIME
AND OTHER MAJOR PRODUCTIONS
IN SEARCH OF COMIC RELIEF
Rachel Gathercole

Trust me: there is no worse experience on the entire planet than taking a bath. I have this from a very reliable source—my son, who over the first few years of his life experienced far more than his share of screaming and crying fits while I attempted to wash his desperately filthy hair. (Sometimes even *he* screamed and cried.)

Fortunately, I have since discovered an amazing secret. An *invaluable* secret. A secret which has brought patience to my parenting and peace to my home. I cannot figure out why it isn't written in every parenting book on the shelves, because it works like a charm. Luckily, I have had the good fortune to learn it directly from my two children, now seven and three. I am talking about nothing less than a golden trump card of early-childhood parenting: *silliness.*

Oh, silliness. Glorious silliness. The things I have accomplished with you that I could never have accomplished any other way! Silliness is pure magic. On even the most difficult of days, it can melt my kids' resistance in an instant and miraculously inspire them to cooperate. All I have to do is muster the creativity. The more resistant they are, the more I know they need the help of the "S" word. Now that I have this tool in my proverbial bag of tricks, I could not raise my kids without it.

Once I made this incredibly helpful discovery, all sorts of bizarre and miraculous things started to happen in our house. All kinds of unusual people began to appear in my stead. Take, for instance, the Clumsy Waitress.

Thanks to my clever friend Annie Collins (the original Clumsy Waitress), our Clumsy Waitress (who bears a striking resemblance to Yours Truly) often shows up at bathtime, instantly transforming the tub into an exciting restaurant, where the food is superb, the beverages invisible, and the well-meaning, lovable waitress forever spilling cups of water on people's heads, smearing (very shampoo-like) pancake syrup on their hair, and dropping slippery bars of (soapy) ice cream on their bellies. Somehow, the children forgive her these klutzy errors and, miraculously, they end up clean.

On other days there is Brunhilda, a friendly, quirky woman who believes children cannot do simple tasks such as soaping themselves, rinsing themselves, and drying off. My kids delight in proving her wrong. Very forgetful of past such experiences, Brunhilda never fails to be shocked at their baffling abilities and usually attributes their accomplishments to the help of invisible goblins, which seems to amuse the children to no end.

Occasionally we are visited by Jimbo Jellybelly, a large, jovial fellow who mistakes the children for large potatoes and attempts to scrub them up and make them into soup in the biggest pot of warm water he can find (which is, of course, the bathtub).

In fact, one never knows who will show up. At times it has been Spartacus, a hairdresser who washes and styles their hair in the most unorthodox of fashions; a fellow by the name of Dirty McGee who simply can't stand cleanliness and insists that it be washed off immediately with soap and water (he showed up on a day when the children did not feel they were dirty enough for a bath); and hungry washcloths in search of a bite of dirt to eat. More than once we have enjoyed the company of Amelia Bedelia, the famous children's-book housekeeper who always misunderstands what she is supposed to do. My children, thoroughly entertained by her misinterpretations, explain the process to her step by step. ("Now rub the shampoo on my hair...no, no, not the whole bottle! Squeeze some out of it first! Silly Amelia Bedelia!") Focused on wording the task carefully so as not to confuse their literalist friend, the kids become partners in accomplishing the task. After she makes a multitude of absurd, laughable mistakes, they are relieved and pleased when Amelia Bedelia finally gets it right and they end up clean.

Of course, skilled as these characters are at smoothing the ride, I don't *always* leave the work to our strange, comical guests. That would hardly be fair, since I, after all, am the mother. So, sometimes I do it myself. Occasionally I will give the children each a handful of shaving cream with which to paint on the tub wall. Distracted from the task at hand, they paint happily, and I wash them. They hardly notice.

Sometimes I ask them to sing a song of their choosing, and we race to see who finishes first—me washing them, or them singing. Other times they count, and see how high they can get before I finish. Somehow in their efforts to win they forget about not wanting to be washed. They don't even mind if I take a while, because the higher they count before I'm done, the more excited they feel. Naturally, they win every time, and then we all ooh and ahh about how high they counted (or how many times they sang the song) before I finished. Then, voila! We get out of the tub and towel off, talking about what story we might read before bed.

The value of this approach, to me, is that it takes the focus off of the undesirable task and puts it onto something they enjoy, while acknowledging that, either way, the task must be done. I like to believe that it teaches my kids self-discipline and positivity (accepting that the task must be done and then finding a positive attitude to do it with). They are free to safely express their negative feelings about taking a bath, and then they also have the option of finding the fun in it and having an enjoyable time. As their mother, I expect them to do what I ask and will help them cooperate and make the task as painless as possible. I love them and want them to have fun.

Their need for me to make these tasks fun is not manipulation. I believe that at ages three and seven they have a legitimate need to be helped through life's distasteful or mundane chores in a way that allows them to feel good about themselves. Perhaps this way they can learn to help themselves through future situations with positivity and the empowerment to find their own ways to enjoy life.

Silliness is certainly a heck of a lot more fun for everyone than nagging, coercing, barking orders, or tearfully submitting to a chore. Play simply averts these power struggles.

In fact, lest I mislead you, I must confess that these antics are in no way limited to bathtime. In our house they start when we wake up in the morning and take us right up to bedtime. After drying off with talking towels that need rescuing from their thirst, and meeting a friendly diaper in search of just the right size toddler to fit on (no one too big or small will do, like Cinderella's slipper), we go to the Fanciest Fancy Clothing Store, which sells exquisite pajamas made of one-of-a-kind silks, the softest of velvets, and sometimes even pure gold. "Madame," the clothier might say, "if you will step this way I will place upon you this fabulous garment, the finest nightgown ever worn by a mortal, normally worth $800,000, but for you, no charge!" The children, thrilled at the privilege, carefully put on the valuable garments. Sometimes they insist on paying, reaching into their invisible pockets and drawing out their million dollar bills ("keep the change") for the occasion.

When it's all over, I suddenly find that (who knew?) everyone is in bed, in their pajamas, clean, with smiling faces and *no tears*. Another successful day, drawn to a close. It's not always a piece of cake, of course. Some days do require every ounce of my creativity. I feel it is well spent.

But that is the exception. When all is said and done, my children like to cooperate. Many days, all that is required is for me to ask them to do something, and they will do it. Still, they are human, and some days it is harder for them. On these days, they need a little more. They need fun. They don't ask a lot—just a little bit of effort on my part to make a disagreeable chore the slightest bit amusing. They are willing to meet me halfway and be amused by anything. They just want a little help.

I am aware that life will be full of unpleasant circumstances and I won't always be there to help them through it. I like to think that I am teaching and fortifying them to find the good in every situation, and to find ways to enjoy life whatever it may throw their way.

For right now, we'll do it together. We'll rise each morning with a grin and a confident attitude that I know from experience can help us through even the most difficult days of motherhood and life: Stand back, world, here we come! We've got a sense of humor, and we know how to use it.

Rachel Gathercole is a freelance writer and the breastfeeding, co-sleeping, sling-wearing, home-birthing, home-schooling mother of two children, ages eight and four. Her articles and essays on motherhood, children, and related topics have appeared in numerous national and local publications. She resides with her husband and children in North Carolina, where she continues to make her way on the incredible journey of motherhood.

PARENTING WITH LOVE AND RESPECT
Katherine Rolls-Carson

It's funny how one's perspective on parenting choices changes with personal experience.

I, for one, admittedly thought my best friend was absolutely out of her mind to sleep in bed with her infant daughter and to respond immediately to her cries. I was one of those uninformed (okay, I'll admit it, "ignorant") and judgmental people who tsk-tsked at those who shared a family bed and responded immediately to their child's cries. In my mind, I thought, "Wow, are they ever going to regret bringing their baby to bed with them. They will never get any sleep, their daughter will never want to go to her own bed, she will cry to get whatever she wants and will never be independent." I, of course, thought I had the right answer, you know, just to put her into her crib, and let her fuss/cry until she settled down and learned to sleep "where she should" and when she should.

Fast-forward a year or so, and my oh-so-short-sighted views changed in an instant! I am the lucky and proud mother of our daughter, born on Valentine's Day of 2002. I had a medication-free delivery and nursed her within thirty minutes of her birth. Our doula and family doctor were fabulous, and I am happy with my birth experience. We stayed in the hospital for about thirty hours, but I just wanted to be home with this enchanting little soul, with whom I felt instantly and completely connected. The plans were for Ella to sleep in a bassinet on my side of the bed for a few months, and then transition into her crib, which was set up in her room before her birth. The first night she came home, I put her into the bassinet and listened anxiously to be sure she was breathing (I know I'm not the only mom to do that!). I couldn't see her, though. So, I picked her up, snuggled her into bed beside me, following the safe co-sleeping guidelines I'd read about while pregnant, but never *dreamed* I'd actually use. Ah, peace! Not only could I hear her breathing, but I also could see her and feel her movements as she slept.

My husband and I have never looked back, and we have such positive feelings about sharing our bed with our child. It is very difficult to pinpoint exactly what I like best about our sleeping arrangement. The proximity promotes awareness of her health; I awaken if she has a fever, or before she is ill, or if she is in some sort of discomfort. It also makes breastfeeding even easier and lets me get more sleep than if I had to get her up, nurse her, ease her back into another sleeping spot, and then head back to bed myself. Actually, we get more sleep this way—she just latches on, and we both fall asleep again!

Aside from practical motivations, however, there are other joys, such as waking up to the most glorious smile in the morning, as Ella opens her eyes to see the two people she loves and trusts most in the world beside her. There's the thrill of feeling little fingertips caressing your cheek, pointing to your nose (accompanied by an early version of the word "nose"), patting the breast as she moves to nurse, and the loving smile I can see in her eyes as she looks up at me. I can only imagine how comforting it must be for her, to know that her parents love and respect her and are sensitive to her needs, responding to them, no matter what the time of day or night.

We have three slings in our house: two mommy-sized, and one Ella-sized (for her stuffed animals). Ella has spent a lot of time in her slings (and also in a front-carrier with daddy). I got my first sling when she was several months old. I love the convenience of it, again, the proximity, the increased opportunities to communicate, and the fact that it enables her to see the world from a birds-eye view. The ease of nursing in the sling cannot be topped (once we got the hang of it), and the simple inclusion of her into my daily activities and interactions is invaluable. There were, of course, detractors (as I was before I had her), who have informed me in their knowing tones of voice that she would never be independent, would become too attached, would not walk on time because we held her too much, and would be "spoiled." I firmly disagree, and I share my reasons, including valid research and personal experiences. I defend my choices and acknowledge that others have made their own.

My now eighteen-month-old daughter is an ambassador for attachment parenting: she demonstrates that she has a great deal of confidence to meet new people and new situations, she makes full advantage of her motor skills to explore, she is happy and bright, and she has many, many words. She is comfortable to express her needs and is able to wait if need be, knowing that she can trust us to address them and honor them as soon as we can. We do set limits on her activities if we feel they are potentially harmful or inappropriate. She will be an active, contributing member of our family—responding to her needs does not equate to letting her always have her way. I believe in gentle discipline, which will help Ella to develop a moral and interpersonal barometer that will serve her well throughout her life.

I believe that our parenting practices of co-sleeping, baby wearing, breastfeeding, and gentle discipline have given Ella an emotional and psychological head start in a society that expects children to be self-sufficient and independent too quickly. I cherish the smiles, hugs, cuddles, giggles, and yes, even the acrobatic nursing sessions, because I know that this part of her life is all too brief, and that, soon, she will be off to explore and conquer the world in her own ways. I know that all of these experiences will contribute to her developing into a loving, sensitive, responsible, and compassionate woman. I want her to have the confidence to express what she needs in life, to know that it is her right to have her needs met, and to be responsive to the needs of others.

Oh, and, yes, I have given my best friend kudos on many occasions for being a sensitive, attached parent!

Katherine Rolls-Carson writes: *I am a professional woman, wife, and mother, and am truly blessed.*

GIFTS

Lynnea Weissman

Three weeks following the birth of my daughter Maya, I received an unsolicited gift. I became suddenly unemployed. The large balloon of public funding, inflated by outrage over OJ Simpson, had slowly deflated. And the Domestic Violence Agency, where I worked, ceased to run.

Depressed about the lost opportunity to save the world, I drifted into a sea of self-pity and aimlessness. What about my career? What about my title? What would my successful friends say at my high school reunion? My life raft was my new baby. Cheered by the cuddly naps, walks with Maya in the backpack imitating bird calls, and countless hours spent reading to her, I slowly began to find importance in the little things.

Desperate to find work, I searched the newspapers, interviewed daycares, and networked with contacts. Programmed from birth to grow up to be *something*, I had always been taught that my self-concept lay in my title and pay scale. I remembered what my father told me when I graduated from college: "In our family, we are leaders, not followers, chiefs, not Indians." How could he be proud of me now?

I went to my first interview with a huge knot in my stomach. How was Maya sleeping? Would she drink from a bottle? Did she miss me? Somehow those infinite two hours passed for both of us, and words couldn't describe the joy I felt upon returning home, seeing those sparkly blue eyes the same as I had left them.

The offer came. Could I line up childcare? Could I wean her to a bottle? By then it was too late. The gift of parenting was a gift I could not surrender. My ego told me to take the job, but

35

somehow my heart overruled. I wanted to raise Maya. I wanted to be the face she saw when she looked up after eating, the voice she heard while falling asleep, the warm body she snuggled against to keep warm, and the person who kissed the tears away when she scraped her knee. I turned the offer down.

I barely caught my breath while the three months that I had planned to take off stretched into six, then nine. Finances were an issue. So I began to look after my friends' kids so that they could keep their careers and titles. I felt resentful and embarrassed about my demotion from "World Saver" to "Childcare Provider." Surrounded by other children's poop, making macaroni and cheese, and playing ring around the rosy, my life's vision collided with the harsh reality of raising toddlers. Around my daughter's first birthday, it finally sunk in. I had traded in my days of power lunches, intern-training, and salary-collecting for the privilege of raising my own daughter.

Although I still pine for my days of glory, I suppose that I have reached a state of equilibrium. Every day gifts await me. The gift of watching Maya learn to ride her bike without training wheels. The gift of sitting with my son as he sneezed through his first flu. The daily gifts of kisses, tears, sharing inside giggles, and lessons learned the hard way that I would not trade for the world.

And over the years I have come to accept that my gift to the world is not ending homelessness or discovering the cure for cancer. I proudly offer my gifts of home-cooked meals, snuggles, shoe-tying lessons, and potty-training. The gift I lovingly give is the gift of being important in the lives of children.

Lynnea Weissman is the mother of two, and caregiver of many.

ATTACHMENT PARENTING, NATURALLY

Josie Bradley

The one truth I have learned is that my parenting style is not better, moral, or the "right way." As I grow as a mother, I have come to see clearly that my method of parenting does not mean I love my children more or less than the next mother. I parent the way I do because my own instinct tells me how to raise my children. My mother did not raise me the way I raise my children. I did not read a book and say, "That is the way to go." In fact, I did not know the phrase "attachment parenting" until my first-born son was three years old. I am lucky enough to have a husband who agrees with my instincts, as well as a wonderful circle of friends who either parent similarly or accept me the way I am without judgment. I have discovered how important this is. I call it my "network." We need to support each other in this experience, the most agony and the most ecstasy one could ever experience.

When my first baby boy was born in a hospital under the knife, I vowed to listen very intently to my mother-voice. My birth had been taken from me; my voice had been taken from me. I woke up from that experience and tuned into myself. There was never the slightest question of circumcising my perfect boy. Was it my right to say whether he would have unnecessary cosmetic surgery at such a young age? I did not think so. His body was in my care to protect. If he wanted to have his foreskin removed as an adult then he should be the one to make that choice. I remember waiting in the hospital with my son and being told not to sleep with my baby or let him fall asleep nursing. Where was this absurd if well-meaning advice coming from? I listened only to myself. This was my gift, my time to

37

mother. I nursed him to sleep for three years. He was and remains a very happy, well-rounded child. My husband and I have two beds set up side by side in our room. My oldest son is now eight and has just recently moved into his own bed for the entire night.

My daughter was born at home three years later. It was then that I fell madly in love with my body. I did it. I had a powerful VBAC home birth. I gave birth standing up. I was so powerful, the earth moved. The night I gave birth, I lay in bed and read my son his bedtime story with his new sister nestled at my breast. There was no separation. It was bliss. I nursed her until she was two. I think she would be nursing to this day, but I was pregnant with number three at the time and my body was tired. Self-care, I have discovered, is the secret to a healthy mother. I give huge amounts to my children, but we have attained balance, more or less, over the years.

By the time my third son was born at home, we were well underway with our parenting lives. Again, the transition was a natural one. We just continued. I think the very best advice I ever received was from my mother. She told me once that "being a mother is this much out of your life," as she held up her fingers an inch apart. I look at my eight-year-old and see what she means. Now I understand the truth of that old famous phrase "they grow up so fast." Why is it that we feel the need to push the process? I want to savor every moment with my children. I want to co-sleep and nurse for as long as my body will allow. My third baby has just turned two and is still nursing. In my heart, there is nothing more sacred and special than bathing those mucky faces, snuggling in bed, and nursing my baby to sleep after a long day of reading, blackberry-picking and eating good food. How much more rich could my life be? I cannot imagine another experience more life affirming than raising children.

Our family will soon add another member, and we are over the moon with happiness. I will carry on with this wonderful gift I have been given. My children and my mother-voice, strong and wild. We are creatures lusting after life. Each day we plan little and live a lot. I have the fortune of being able to realize my wish, raising and schooling my children at home. I have recently made the discovery of downtime. This is really important stuff. More important than doing, we are simply being. There is plenty of time to be busy. Right now we are here. This is our place and I do not want to miss a beat. Soon enough my children will be grown and off on their own. What will I do with myself, I wonder...Then I remember: "*Grandchildren!!!*"

Josie Bradley *is a mother of three children, expecting her fourth. She has naturally fallen onto the path of attachment parenting, finding in it the joy of motherhood.*

PARENTING FROM THE HEART
A PERSONAL STORY OF ATTACHMENT PARENTING
Natalie Cresitello

Before I had a child, I considered myself an average American woman, very much like my peers in terms of my childrearing beliefs. Once my daughter was born, however, I discovered how different I really was. The parenting advice I received from friends and some family did not seem appropriate. I could not accept that crying was "good" for my baby, and that I needed to teach her to "self-soothe" so early in her life. I started to wonder who these people were, and I quickly looked for a new peer group. Luckily, in the Mother's Group at the Lactation Resource Center (in nearby Chatham, New Jersey), I found comfort and reassurance that I was not alone in my parenting philosophy and that this philosophy even had a name—attachment parenting.

My daughter was what my husband and I call a "needy" baby from the start. She would only sleep in my arms (day and night) and would wake up screaming the second I would try to put her down. Even when she was awake, she wanted to be held all the time. She nursed frequently—every one to two hours or more—and would never accept a bottle. I received criticism from friends and family that I was spoiling her, because I accommodated her wishes on demand. As a new mother, I was unsure that I was doing the right thing, but in my heart I felt that loving my baby and answering her needs could not be damaging her. I was even accused of being insecure, thus encouraging my baby to "need me." There were so many times that others' criticisms had me second-guessing myself, but I stood my ground and continued to follow my heart. Now, sixteen months later, I am so happy I did.

41

Once my daughter became mobile (she started crawling at six months and walking at ten months), she was a much happier baby and became much less needy. She loved to explore on her own, secure in the fact that I was nearby and accessible if she needed me. At one year, my husband and I moved her out of our bed and into her own (a twin mattress on the floor). She likes to sleep by herself now, but if and when she calls out to me, I always go to her. To be honest, I still love sleeping with her nestled beside me. There is nothing more wonderful than the face of a peaceful, sleeping baby. I feel sorry for mothers who never get to experience this bliss.

My husband and I always joked that our daughter would be sleeping with us until she left for college or got married. Now we see how quickly she is growing up and becoming independent. Sometimes I realize it will not be long before she reaches other milestones in her life, like weaning. I know she has gradually been outgrowing so many of her favorite comforts, and this may well be next. All the things I once worried so much about—creating a dependent child, a poor sleeper, a spoiled brat—now seem so ridiculous to me. My daughter is none of these things. She is a happy, well-adjusted, and pretty fearless toddler. She is growing up, like all babies do.

I am so happy with the way that I am raising my daughter and with the results I see. I have and will always let her decide when she is ready to take the next step in her life, whether it is sleeping alone, weaning, or just being away from me for a while. It is certainly not easy to practice attachment parenting—it takes a lot of time, patience and love. But thanks to this parenting style, my daughter and I have a bond like nothing else I have ever known. We are seldom apart—by choice, not need—and neither of us would have it any other way. And one day, when she is all grown up and miles away from me, I know we will still be inseparable in our bond and our hearts.

Natalie Cresitello, with a BA in mathematics and secondary education credentials, is currently the stay-at-home mother of two daughters, ages two and a half years and two and a half months. She resides with her family in Berkeley Heights, New Jersey.

Always Together—My Son and Me
The Story of an Attached Mama
Tiffany Palisi

I have never been one to stray far from my loved ones. I've always taken "family vacations," with the exception of one spring break trip and two snowboarding excursions. This was by choice. I've never liked leaving my family behind.

I lived in my parents' home until I was married, and even then I've always lived within seven miles of their home. My grandparents and my brother both live one town away. I cannot imagine moving to a different state, much less a different country. I admire the adventurers who tour Europe on their own, going from one youth hostel to another with nothing more than a map and a Eurail pass in hand, but I never actually desired to do so myself. I like having the comfort of my family nearby.

My son has been within earshot of me from the very start. He roomed with me at the hospital and it was magnificent. I had a private room that allowed my husband, Johnny, to sleep in the room with us. He was sleeping on a cot, my son was sleeping in my arms, and while I watched the snow fall gently from the sky, I smelled the sweet breath of my newborn child and was transformed into a mother. We have not been separated since. I have had many offers for babysitting from lovely, trustworthy people, free of charge, and my husband would gladly take care of our son if I wanted to go shopping or to the gym. It is just not something I am interested in—leaving him, that is.

I have chosen to write about this because I feel a great deal of societal pressure is being put on mothers to leave their babies. At my six-month checkup with my former midwife, I found that she was horrified to hear that I had never left my son alone. She "prescribed" that I go to dinner and a movie with my husband and "have some wine," sans baby. Feeling attacked by her unwarranted demand while also feeling a bit unsure about my position, I asked my husband how he felt about this. He merely said, "We decided to have a baby so that we could have a family. We can still be a couple while John Henry is in our company. I think her telling us how to live our personal life is ridiculous."

Since that time, we have been invited to two weddings, bringing more pressure to leave our son. When I mentioned that the travel and the hours didn't work for our son, the hosts' replies were similar: "So, just get a babysitter." Yes, easy and common enough, just not something I wished to do. At this point in my life, I know there is no greater joy than being with my son. If he weren't with me, I believe that I would do nothing but miss him. That's not fun at all.

In this life, we have a certain amount of time to spend with our children before they go off to school, then perhaps to college (or to backpack Europe), and embark on their lives independent of us. I'm constantly stopped by mothers of college-aged kids who, when seeing John Henry in the sling, begin to cry. The most recent one said, "Oh, when my daughter was his age, I grudgingly held her if she wouldn't go in the stroller. All I did was complain about her always clinging to me. Now she's in college and I'd give anything to do it all over. You're lucky you realize how fleeting babyhood is." I do feel lucky that I can be a stay-at-home mother, and I enjoy nearly every moment I have of my son's childhood. Soon, he will be out enjoying his friends and his newfound freedom.

To compare this attachment to the one I have with my husband, let me share a story with you. I met my husband nine years ago. From the moment we met, we haven't been apart for more than a few days. He never had or wanted a boys' night out; I never had or wanted a girls' night out. We both wanted to be together. We spent one night each weekend with another couple whom we love dearly, Tom and Andrea. Even when Johnny and I weren't getting along so well, we always preferred each other's company to anyone else's; sometimes that meant that he and Tom watched television in one room while Andrea and I talked in another. Other times, we sat in silence, which was okay, too. We were still able to hug one another or share a smile at a moment's notice. And that was very important to me.

Sitting at his parent's home one night in the company of his mother, who had devastatingly lost her husband to a heart attack a few years before, a family friend asked if we ever got sick of each other. My reply was, "Sometimes, but never so much so that I don't want to be around him. Every day together is a gift." His mother responded, "That's right." Having lost the one person she chose to spend her life and grow brilliantly old with, she completely understood how I felt.

I, too, know that in a flash I could lose any one of the people I love, and that is what makes love so sacred. Life is all a luxurious gift. I want to share it with those I love.

During a recent blackout, now called the Blackout of 2003, many people I knew were stuck in New York City. They lived just across the water in Hoboken but couldn't get across—the trains weren't running and the lines for buses and boats were hours long. All I could think about was what would happen to a mother who needed to get home to her nursling and couldn't. What would this child think and feel? How panicked would the mother be (as I know I would be)? Then I looked back at my son, sitting in his car seat as we drove home, thankful that we were together. I believe that this is part of what keeps me so physically close to him. I know how much he needs me, and I don't believe that anything is worth the cost of being separated.

About a year ago, some friends whose company I really enjoy had a girls' night out. Their babies stayed with their husbands while they went to dinner. I hadn't been out of the house for seven days, as my son was suffering with a horrible virus, and I felt it was important for me to always be with him, especially when he was not feeling well. But by that seventh day, the same day my friends were meeting for dinner, the invitation to join them was tempting. I hadn't had a moment to myself, even to go to the bathroom, and I was thoroughly drained. Then I looked down at my little son, standing in pants far too big for him and looking tiny in our cluttered kitchen, his starry green-blue eyes staring up at me through his amber-colored bangs, and I thought, No, it's just not for me.

Tiffany Palisi is the proud mother of John Henry who, at two and a half years old, loves co-sleeping, nursing, and riding in the sling. She functions as a NOCIRC (National Organization of Circumcision Information Resource Centers) center and loves educating people on natural attachment parenting.

MOTHERHOOD

Jeanine Ketch

Motherhood: a sweet privilege and gift in my life. I was a well-loved, scheduled, bottle-fed, put-to-sleep-in-my-own-bed kind of child. I was eager to please, easygoing, compliant, never really questioning the "rules" or what was considered to be the "norm." The journey of motherhood has taken me from a single-minded woman, whose intent was to obtain a doctorial degree in special education, to an open-minded, stay-at-home mom, whose intent is to listen to her own inner voice (sometimes with a struggle, other times with ease) and to connect with her children.

Our five wonderful children have guided me toward the pull of my inner wisdom. They have enabled me to listen to and trust what I believe is inside every woman: a "resource" waiting to be discovered. This journey has not, by any means, made me into the "perfect" mom. We have encountered many bumps along the way, made huge mistakes, and sometimes allowed external influences and pressures to hush that inner wisdom. I found it helpful to seek the support of like-minded women and families in several incredible La Leche League groups. Supportive information from books like *The Womanly Art of Breastfeeding*, *Mothering Your Nursing Toddler*, *Nighttime Parenting*, and *Baby Catcher* has also been helpful. It is just a matter of finding the balance, watching and listening to the cues, then readjusting to what works best for our family.

One of the first memorable moments, in which I listened to my inner voice and connected with my child, was in my last month of my first pregnancy, at a routine OB-GYN office visit.

The doctor examined me (obviously not hearing a word I was saying), and very matter-of-factly he said, "I will see you next week." I walked out of that office laughing to myself. Six short hours later, I was holding my beautiful first-born son.

On a similar, but sad note, in my fourth pregnancy I called the doctor's office because I felt, but did not want to believe, that our baby had left us at the very young age of eight weeks' gestation. The nurse told me coldly that my hormones had me off-balance and to enjoy feeling good, that each pregnancy was different and that you don't always feel morning sickness or feel tired or tender-breasted. (All these glorious sensations had been present and then abruptly had stopped.) One week later, our miscarriage began. My body mourned with recurrent sensations of my milk letting down for weeks. This child is celebrated each Easter (the due date) with an ever-growing spring flower bulb garden.

We have been fortunate along this journey to be able to put each of our newborns to the breast soon after their natural births, keeping them close, establishing our exclusive breastfeeding relationships. Nurturing, on demand, my children's physical and emotional needs at my breast is a glorious step in this journey that has truly intensified my connection with my children. I have been questioned about being a human pacifier. I am at peace knowing that seeking comfort from contact with people over an object is incomparable. (Just what do they think those artificial nipples are modeled after, anyway?)

Another revelation in our journey has been our sleeping arrangements. We had been given a crib as a gift in 1986 and took great time and effort in setting it up, picking out the "perfect" bedding to prepare a sleeping haven for the arrival of our first baby. After night awakenings, fumbling to get to my baby quickly, and the louder and louder shouts of my inner voice (not to mention the need for sleep), finally I put my children in their truly "perfect" bed: our family bed. What a comfort the warmth and smell is, how soothing it is to look at their peaceful faces, breastfeed easily and on demand, and feel on my cheek and heart the soft breath of my children throughout the night. It makes getting out of bed difficult some mornings.

But that's where the baby wearing begins; in frontpacks, backpacks, or a sling, whichever the situation calls for. We have worn babies doing daily routines, shopping, hiking, camping, attending public and school events, swimming, traveling, moving across the country (several times), walking the beaches of New Hampshire, Florida, Alabama and North Carolina, even caving. Could this be overindulgence or spoiling? I've been asked this on many occasions. I know from within that spoiling only occurs when something is neglected or untouched. Could all this baby wearing be creating an overly dependent child? Again I'm reassured that fully and naturally meeting the needs of my child will produce a well-adjusted, secure, and independent adult.

Motherhood: a journey that has allowed me to question, to grow, and to connect with my family in ways I never imagined. It is wonderful, exhausting at times, exhilarating most of the time, and treasured—an extraordinary parent-child dance!

Jeanine Ketch is a stay-at-home mom of five children, four living boys (ages sixteen, fifteen, twelve, and three) who were exclusively breastfed. She has been a La Leche League Leader for one year and aspires to someday be a doula.

Writer's Block

Abigail Dotson

Eighteen months into my daughter's life, I sat down to write. About something. Anything. Two years ago, I had considered myself a writer. I knew that having a baby would mean less time to write; I anticipated tired bones dragging an aching body to the computer at three in the morning after a midnight feeding, or disregarding the pile of dirty dishes in the sink for twenty minutes with the keyboard during the baby's afternoon nap. I had a romantic notion of an affair with my typewriter, finding each other in darkened hallways and spending a passionate five minutes touching, our time together always abruptly ending before we were ready. I knew I would be bursting with words, searching for outlets in each of my ten fingers; I imagined sleepless nights prolonged by an unrelenting urge to write wild fairytales that I would sprinkle with glitter and bind in a book for her sweet eyes to peruse as she grew.

I thought that although the time would be sparse and of course I would never get to write everything I wanted, I would grasp those precious moments of peace with unheard-of gusto, filling pages with drawings and poems and stories and other such craftiness. Never before had I had reason for such inspiration; the coming months would provide me with a wealth of creative fire, which I would put out little by little in the stolen minutes while she was napping or frolicking with her father. Imagination had been my buoy through life so far, keeping me afloat during even the most vicious of storms. I had felt love and death and brokenness travel through my blood and limbs to exit on a page of often-sappy poetry and stories. And so, of course, in this most momentous time I was sure to be filled with such ideas, the likes of which I had never experienced.

So I knew there would be little time, maybe even no time. I was prepared to feel frustrated and loaded with a traffic jam of creative genius. What nobody told me, what I didn't anticipate, was the complete lack of creative genius I actually felt. In all the classes and books and conversations with authentic mothers, no one ever told me that writer's block was a possible side effect of giving birth.

Those first few weeks when I sat down to excitedly to write the story of my daughter's birth (an absolutely perfect night), I was shocked to find myself afflicted with writer's block. For the first time in my life, I had nothing to say. But how could this be? Perhaps more than any other time in my life, there was so much to say. And yet time and time again I hurried to the computer, anxious to let the prose flow, only to sit paralyzed. I eked out miserable paragraphs, struggling with each sentence and never feeling fulfilled. I imagined my daughter reading these colorless words in the years to come and felt robbed of the gift I always assumed I would give her. The mother I was in my dreams recorded her first maternal days in a lively and dedicated journal, but I was quick to find out that we can't all be Anne Lamott.

It seemed that raising a child, at least a newborn, was in and of itself such a creative trial that there was nothing left over. And I had (read: *had*) a relatively easy baby. She was mostly happy; she slept peacefully nestled next to me, waking often but only to nurse and fall back into dreams. Friends and family were constantly around, feeding us and taking turns admiring her infantness. I was happy—elated, even—adrenaline-pumped, but still tired (although looking back on those days, I think, crazily enough, not as tired as I am now). I was perhaps steeped in delusion, filled with a Wonder Woman-like feeling that not only would I, *should* I, raise this little baby of mine, but I would also write beautiful stories and poems and adventure tales. In my postpartum craziness, I didn't realize that I was spent. The hours of rocking and walking, of singing sweet lullabies and silly songs, of conversations where I was the only one talking—this was where my real poetry was written. The experience was not so dull and uninspiring as to neglect provocation of creative endeavor, nor was I suddenly transformed into such a dull and uninspiring person as to inhibit imagination. I was simply redefining it for myself. Temporarily.

Eighteen months later, I am only beginning to find words again. I am just starting to call myself a writer. I feel the spark again, deep in my gut, like an old friend I am so happy to let back in the door. My daughter still takes up most of my time. At eighteen months, she runs and plays and sings and talks; we dress up and kick down castles, dump out buckets of water, and take long walks on the beach. There is hardly a moment to get a word down on paper, and sometimes I wait all week for that opening, only to find myself at a loss for words once again. But sometimes, when she has slept well the night before and had a relatively peaceful morning, she may fall asleep for an afternoon nap and I may have just enough energy to forgo the nap and snuggle for an hour or two with the keyboard instead.

What I realize is that not only is raising a child all the things that everyone tells you: it is also an art form. Raising my daughter, right now, for me, is an art. I paint her and mold her and shape her and write her into each of my own dawns, and then I stand back and admire her as she learns to paint and mold and shape and write herself into each of her own days.

Abigail Dotson writes: *I live in the Santa Cruz Mountains with my nineteen-month-old daughter, Ruby Jane, and her papa. Most days we spend frolicking under a canopy of redwoods and hunting banana slugs. Sometimes we find a poem hidden in the trees or on the road; sometimes we find a story; sometimes we just find fun. (Abigail's writing has appeared on www.mothering.com.)*

ATTACHMENT PARENTING
AN ANTIDOTE FOR A HECTIC LIFE
Carla Moquin

My husband, Charlie, and I have a two-year-old daughter named Alpha. I work full time as a secretary in a large law firm, and I am in my third year of an online law school. Because of financial needs, I needed to return to work part time when Alpha was only four weeks old. Happily, we found a wonderful family that takes care of her along with their own two children when we're at work, but it was still very difficult to leave my daughter so soon. I had to transition to a full-time work schedule when she was about nine months old.

Given the hectic nature of my life, I can't imagine how I would have remained sane had I not nursed her, co-slept with her until very recently, and used a sling nearly constantly until she lost interest in it at around eight months old. Nursing and co-sleeping allowed me to establish a close bond with her, even though I had to work out of the house, and I'm convinced that it helped her cope better with those times when she wasn't with my husband or me.

The sling went everywhere we did. Both Charlie and I wore it frequently. He was great at arranging a blanket under her tiny head so she was secure in the sling but could still see what was going on. As she got old enough to sit up, I would put her Indian-style in the sling, facing out. Very rarely did she cry while in the sling, since it kept her in close proximity to a parent, and at the same time, she was able to enjoy the scenery. Because she felt secure, she was able to focus on experiencing and learning about the world. I actually looked forward to grocery shopping with her. She felt so cozy in the sling, and my hands were free to pick up items and point things out to her. I once won a game of miniature golf one-handed while nursing her in the sling during most of the game; that's when my friends really started to appreciate just how useful a sling was. We took her to parties with large groups of adults. She would hang out in the sling on either me or my husband the whole time. Even at a few months old, she loved parties because she met lots of interesting people and never had to wonder where her parents were. Using a sling made it easy for us to integrate her into our social lives instead of having to forgo adult contact or leave her with a sitter if we wanted to go see some friends. It also allowed her to learn about social interactions instead of being left at home or stuck in a baby carrier all the time.

When she was an infant, breastfeeding made our lives wonderfully easy. Her diaper bag contained nothing but an extra outfit, diapers, and wipes; I never had to worry about bottles. If she got hungry when we were out, it was easy to shift her position in the sling so that she could nurse discreetly while I continued shopping or doing other things. Nursing helped her work through bad moods, because it provided food, touch, and comfort at the same time. She could be screaming and miserable, but if I nursed her, a few minutes later she'd be cheery and acting as though she had never been upset. My husband commented many times that nursing seemed to reset her happiness gauge. She and I took frequent trips throughout her babyhood, and she was a model child on planes because if her ears started to hurt or she was tired, I could easily and quickly nurse her, which relieved airplane-induced ear pressure, visibly calmed her down, and allowed her to gently and quickly fall sleep if she was tired. I had dozens of strangers come up to me after plane trips to tell me they couldn't believe how well-behaved and content she was. We've been on at least twenty planes since she was born, and she has always done extremely well, mostly due to the soothing power of nursing. We still nurse in the morning and evening because it continues to comfort her. It still resets her happiness gauge.

I pumped milk for her from the time I first went back to work until she was a year and a half old. Once I got into a rhythm, it was easy, and the cost of the pump and effort involved was still way better than dealing with formula would have been. We co-slept from the day of her birth. In the hospital, she slept on my chest, which was an absolutely incredible feeling. Because I didn't have to get out of bed to feed or comfort her, I slept great, even during those nights when she woke up frequently. My husband slept even better, since he never had to get up to make her formula. One of the coolest things about nursing is that you don't have to fully wake up to do it. I could just get her latched on and fall right back to sleep. She slept better because her parents were there, and I wasn't a sleep-deprived zombie like most other new moms I've known. As she approached two, we transitioned her to sleeping on her own, and she's doing great with it. From being so close to us in her early months, I believe that she now has confidence that we're there if she really needs us, and so she is able to sleep securely by herself. She has even taken to shutting her bedroom door in the morning, indicating that she is enjoying having a private room.

When the inevitable clashes between parent and child occur, nursing allows us to easily reestablish our bond. I feel that I can be more effective in teaching her what is and is not acceptable behavior, because I am not afraid of making her temporarily angry with me. Because of the bond that our parenting style has created between her and us, I believe that she always knows on a basic level that we love her and want the best for her, and that makes her more willing to do things that make us happy.

Working and having a child is a complex balance, but I enjoy being productive and having a rewarding work life. For me, being productive in my job replenishes my energy, and I think it makes me a better parent. I cherish every moment I am able to spend with my daughter (and my husband). I never get tired of Alpha or feel as though taking care of her is a chore. I sometimes feel bad that I can't be with her more, but overall, I think working outside the home improves my ability to be patient with her and appreciate of the time we have. And our attachment parenting methods allow me to maintain a close connection with her even though I spend time away from her.

Alpha is now a confident, energetic, happy, healthy, affectionate, well-behaved little girl. She loves meeting new people. Though there are some things I want to do slightly differently with any subsequent children we may have, nursing, co-sleeping, and using a sling are things that are definitely going to be a part of how we raise them.

Carla Moquin *is married and a mother to a two-year-old girl. She works at Snell & Wilmer, a large law firm, as a floater legal secretary. She is in her third year at Concord University, a year-round, four-year, fully online law school. She and her husband grew up on the East Coast and currently live in Salt Lake City, Utah.*

CONNECTING
Carolyn M. Klabin

My daughter, Tiffany, is an attached parent. Tiffany says I, too, am attached. An attached grandmother. Being an "attached grandmother" encompasses many descriptions. I've never read a technical description of this title nor do I know if one exists; I'm not concerned about it. I'm too busy enjoying my time with the joyous being who is my grandson, John Henry. His name alone makes me happy. I know that millions of grandparents feel the way I do, but I think what puts attached grandparents in a different category from the "average" lucky grandparent is that our daughters (or daughters-in-law) are attached mamas, carrying their babies constantly. When Tiffany told me of her decision to keep John Henry with her (or with Daddy) at all times, I was happy and supportive.

Twenty-eight years ago, I had the same philosophy with Tiffany's little brother, Justin, after hearing anthropologist Ashley Montague speak, and then reading his mind-altering book called Touching. Its reasoning and information, backed up by research stating the great benefits of constantly holding one's infant, made me an ardent and determined convert to this "radical" motherhood. I nursed him on demand, and he ended up sleeping in our bed because he'd cry incessantly in the little bassinet next to our bed, only stopping when he slept with us. (Topping the list of the very few regrets I have in my life is the fact that I never nursed Tiffany more than a few days, because the nurse told me she was starving, and that I never put her in bed with us as an infant.) The positive aspect of my regret is that Tiffany is redeeming my mothering mistakes by her compassionately conscious rearing of John Henry. By all accounts, I was the most "radical" mom among my peers, having my son in bed with us. Tiffany, at five years old, was in and out of our bed, which we took apart—laying a king-size mattress on our bedroom floor. This arrangement worked out well. We never worried about the baby falling out of bed. I never used the Baby Bjorn-type carrier that was available to me because you'd wear it on your back, and that meant that I couldn't see or monitor my baby. Daily activities were a challenge, at times, but I got very strong all the same.

Although I had no familial role models for nursing and attached parenting, I received lots of help from my local La Leche League. I received criticism from certain friends, yet I stood my ground. I was the mother tiger and this was my cub. (Tiffany honey, you were my cub, too.) No one could mother my child better than I—that was my philosophy. Because Justin was my second child, I was confident that I knew what was best for my baby.

✳ ✳ ✳ ✳ ✳

Now in 2003, I remember the sweet joy of nursing and feeding my children, yet, to Tiffany's surprise, have no desire to nurse anymore. Nature's natural progression, I believe. Yet I have the same tiger's instinct to nurture and protect my grandson at all costs.

From the day John Henry arrived I felt connected to him. He started crying while Mommy was preparing to nurse. I took him in my arms and started singing to him. He stopped crying. "He likes music," I thought, and thus began my days of rocking John Henry to sleep whenever I could, singing. He was particularly fond of the song "Bali Hai" from the musical South Pacific. I'd continue singing my favorite melodies as I rocked him to sleep while Tiffany showered. Constantly holding my infant grandbaby, who was never out of loving arms unless his diaper was being changed, was tiring at times, but it filled me with a sacred connection that matched no other experience.

All the while, many family members and friends would tell Tiffany to put John Henry down, that "he'd get spoiled," or that she needed to spend time away from her angel. He had lived inside of her for nine months! Why did they need to separate? I became my daughter's advocate. Attached moms face a lot of criticism. A friend even said John Henry wouldn't develop properly by being held so much. Ahem! At eleven months he started walking and talking very well. He liked being upright so much that he started running. Our belief is that because attached babies relate to the world at adult eye level, their skills develop at a faster rate and are more finely tuned. They also look you square in the eye as they study your face. This behavior is generally unlike nonattached, bottle-fed babies' (my blatantly prejudiced statement actually comes from observing numerous babies and toddlers as Tiffany, John Henry, and I participated in music classes and social situations, such as playgroups). This assertion is further reinforced when I see that attached toddlers are calmer and more observant than their unattached peers.

I look at my "Grandlove" as a beautiful and intelligent soul. My experience with him only places him in higher esteem with each passing day. He shows me the depth of his compassion, his thought processes, and his sensitivity in addition to showing me his big muscles as he says, at two and a half years old, "See, Nana, I'm strong." Or when we're riding in the car, John Henry loves the window rolled down, and sometimes it's cold and I prefer it up, so now he'll say, "Nana, you okay?" Concern for my well-being at two and a half! It blows me away. I walk into the living room where he's eating and he says, "Nana, want some grapes?" Generosity. When he was under a year old, he used to cry and get jealous if I held another child. I was flattered and honored, though thankfully, this phase has passed.

Singing together, playing, eating, discovering, on and on—I wish this time could go on forever. I'm here for my grandson, who is a great spirit. He's growing up so fast that I want to witness and share every moment I can with him. The attached parenting philosophy by which Tiffany raises John Henry finds him loving his life. Everything is joy and a party. Throughout our day together he's Bob the Builder, Spider-Man, then Batman, or he's Emeril, saying, "Yeah baby, let's kick it up another notch!" arms raised to the sky. Then he transforms into his old favorite, Buzz

Lightyear, and some days he's Luke Skywalker, if there's anything around resembling a lightsaber. He was playing lightsabers with "Baby," a doll that's John Henry's friend, competitor, alter ego, and often a Huck Finn to his Tom Sawyer. Most recently, John Henry has become Mr. Rogers, Fireman Bill (from Elmo), and Cowboy Jim (a friend of ours). He also does a great Popeye, whose strength expands after he eats his spinach.

It was very heartwarming, yet bittersweet, when John Henry became Daddy Spider-Man today as he told Little Spider-Man, his smaller Spider-Man doll, that he had to leave him and go to work because he had his shoes on. (He does this because when his dad puts on his shoes, because it means he's leaving the house.) He enacts this scenario in various ways throughout our days together, and he often wants to visit Daddy at work. Being with my grandson daily and observing firsthand how he is learning and processing the experiences of his life is fascinating. For a while he was being very independent and telling Tiffany, "You go, Mama," wanting her to leave the room so that he could play alone with me. Within the last week, he's become more attached to Tiffany than usual for no apparent reason. Watching him bounce back and forth from independence is always a surprise.

Above all, I feel being an attached grandmother means supporting my attached daughter in her consciously compassionate method of raising my grandson, loving and respecting him as the intelligent and sensitive human being that he is. It means really listening to him and showing him the respect he deserves, while modeling positive behavior as we both play together. Mostly, though, I follow his lead. John Henry has a strong personality and will, although these days he reserves this behavior for those closest to him. Most of all, he is extremely entertaining and fun.

The other day, while accompanying Tiffany to the skin doctor, I ran into an old tennis friend who was working at the front desk. I happily said my hellos and she asked if I was still playing tennis, as she is. I said I wasn't, and she replied that she said she could see I had better things to do. Then Tiffany said something to John Henry, who was wrapped in her arms in the sling. My tennis friend said, "You talk to him like he's a person." Shocked at this statement, we both said in disbelief, "*He is a person!*" This woman happens to be the mother of two teenage children. Does she know they are people?

I believe that when you are an attached grandparent, from the very start, as you hold your grandbaby as much as possible, you connect with him or her, and you see this baby as a great soul living inside a temporarily tiny body, whose birthright is your constant loving attention and respectful care. Your attached baby will revere you as you revere him, and this way of connecting will produce a bond of unconditional love and respect for the feelings and rights of the other, as well as for others. This connection will provide a sacred imprint that you'll carry together all your lives.

Thank you, Tiffany and John Henry, for giving me Christmas each and every day of my life. I adore you both.

Love, Nana (Mommy)

* * * * *

P.S. The practical reason for attached grandparenting is that there are times during the day when Mommy needs to do various things (showering, cooking dinner), so caring for baby in Nana's arms has allowed Mommy to do these very things.

Carolyn Klabin *was born Carolyn Maria Lanni on September 18, 1947 in Providence, Rhode Island. She is married and the proud mother of Tiffany Palisi and Justin Klabin. She is the adoring grandmother of John Henry Palisi.*

Paving a New Way

Kathleen Lynch

I am glad to have the opportunity to share my parenting choices with other parents because in many ways I have chosen the unpopular road, at least in this culture and within my immediate family, and I want other families who make less popular choices to see that they are not alone. I have found that the more educated I become, the more I see problems with the way things have been done traditionally. The pressures to conform to traditional beliefs and customs are uncomfortable, if not painful.

My story begins with an understanding of where I came from. I am the youngest of five children. Like many families, my father worked full time and my mother stayed home and did most of my rearing. My mother admits that by the time she had me, she was tired of rearing children and she was clinically depressed. Because of this, she did not receive me with the energy and excitement that I deserved. To this day, I struggle with self-blame for the way I was treated. Deep inside, I wonder whether I am lovable. My mother (not to mention my father, who backed her up) had what I believe to be some misguided beliefs in raising children. She left me to cry in the crib alone for long periods of time, not wanting me to "manipulate" her into getting what I wanted or needed. She left some of the rearing to my twelve-year-old sister, who sometimes enjoyed it and other times resented it. When I was angry, my mother got angry back instead of hearing me and addressing my needs before her own. She used some physical violence to discipline me. She has rarely been able to talk with me without saying something that hurts my feelings. She has never been able to say she is sorry for hurting me. It's sad that in our lives together we have never been very close. For a long time, I didn't want children because I didn't want to repeat history. After years of therapy, I felt ready to give at last! I knew I was on the right track when my childrearing values were very different from hers. I knew in my heart that I would be a wonderful, loving mother.

I have made some different choices than what I experienced growing up and what is popular in American culture. I chose to breastfeed and not just for the first year, but for as long as my child needed or wanted it. I am still breastfeeding my daughter, who is two and a half years old. I know through reading all the current literature that it is nutritionally superior to cow's milk for a growing child. I know that it helps soothe and comfort her. It provides a connection between us. It provides antibodies and comfort when she is sick. It has made her colds less severe and she has had few ear infections. I know that breastfeeding helps reduce risk of breast and ovarian cancers, and osteoporosis for the mother. I know that both research and mother's intuition show that there are numerous medical, emotional, and practical benefits for mother, child, and family.

I learned very quickly that it was easier to have the baby sleep in bed with my husband and me so that I could breastfeed on demand and so that the baby would feel secure and not spend time crying alone in the crib. None of us were sleep-deprived after my daughter's birth, and that is one complaint that I hear from many parents of newborns. The research that I read indicates that there is less Sudden Infant Death Syndrome (SIDS) with co-sleeping babies. My husband and I have always been very aware of where the baby is during the night so rolling over on her (what others feared) was not an issue. I know that when my daughter is ready, she will want to sleep in her own room.

I am now pregnant with our second child, who we saw through ultrasound is a boy. Current research indicates that there is no medical reason to circumcise him, so we do not choose to hurt him or risk infection for no good reason. I have been able to breastfeed during pregnancy. I feel some soreness at times but it is not that bad and since I am used to it from having yeast (thrush) in my nipples after her birth, I have learned to tolerate it. One acquaintance accused me of "harming the fetus" by breastfeeding, and that was not only an ignorant comment, but also an insensitive one. I think it's both amazing and aggravating how many people act as if they are authorities when they have not read one bit of current research. I have chosen to tandem-nurse once the baby is born if my toddler still wants to. My parents and sister have given me a hard time about it. At first, it was difficult for me not to have the support of immediate family members for what I believe is a well-thought-out decision. I have come to the conclusion that they just don't get it. One hope I have for this essay is that parents who do make similar choices to mine will see that they are NOT alone, and I hope knowing that, in itself, is a comfort.

As far as birth goes, I had a long first labor in a hospital setting. I was fearful of the pain but knew I wanted to try birthing without medications. Because of hospital policy, I was told to sit still for fifteen to twenty minutes periodically to monitor the baby's heartbeat. It was excruciating to sit still while having labor contractions. I knew I did not want to sit still for my second birth. Late in labor, I had no way of knowing how much longer I would have to deal with the pain and exhaustion, and I didn't think I could hold on any longer without some pain relief and rest. I opted for the epidural, but I do have some regrets that I didn't hold on till the finish. I found that the hospital setting was not relaxing and epidurals were too easy to obtain. I feel angry and disappointed with the medical profession, which seems to treat every birth as if it's high risk. It seems they are too ready to intervene with drugs and surgery which themselves have risks. Many doctors have the women birth on top of a bed in a semi-sitting position, which is convenient for the doctor but not ideal for the mother because there is counter-pressure working against her pelvic outlet. Also, the nurses in the hospital told me when to push because I could not feel the urge to do so as a result of my epidural. They instructed me to push long and hard while holding my breath which, I have come to learn, is a "purple push" or, more technically, "Valsalva maneuver." This is not ideal for the mother or baby for many reasons. I believe that the side effects I got, including hemorrhoids, a swollen perineum that made the birth opening even smaller, tearing, and my bladder dropping, could have been reduced or eliminated if I had been in a better birthing position and had not held my breath for a "purple push."

I do not know exactly how my second birth will go or if there will be any complications, but I can control some things. For example, I chose to birth with midwives in a more relaxed atmosphere. I made accommodations to labor in the comfort of a warm bath. I chose midwives who will support my giving birth in any position that is comfortable to me, not just what is convenient for them. I want to know what it feels like to go through labor and delivery without medication. I want to feel the urge to push. I want to make the best out of this second birth experience and maintain optimal health for myself and baby.

Kathleen Lynch *is a proud mother of one daughter and one son on the way. She is an active member of La Leche League and an avid reader of breastfeeding, birthing, and parenting books.*

BIRTH: BEFORE AND BEYOND

THE LITTLEST DOULA

Pamela Fellner

Our ultimate goal as parents is a common one—to have children who love and appreciate one another. However, our first step towards this goal seemed unusual to many people. As soon as I became pregnant with Shamus, I knew I wanted his three-year-old sister, Brooklyn, to be there for his birth.

My husband, Brian, and I were so happy to be pregnant again, and I felt it so important to give Brook the opportunity to feel the same excitement. Many lazy mornings she and I spent talking about me trying to conceive again. Finally those lazy mornings transformed into amusing moments of her blowing raspberries on my pregnant tummy. So our journey began.

Together we would read childbirth books, studying anatomy diagrams and birthing photographs. I remember her exclaiming, "That little baby needs help getting out, Mama!" And so began our discussion of how moms have contractions and how the baby also has to work to be born. I felt it was important for her to understand that childbirth is not an easy process for moms or babies, though the culmination of efforts is beyond words. She raised some eyebrows at her casual mentions of fetuses, sperms, and umbilical cords (or as she would say, combilical cords). We literally spent hours looking at Sheila Kitzinger's and Lennart Nilsson's childbirth books, her curiosity making it so joyful. I kept teasing that I was going to sign her up as a guest lecturer for our local eighth-grade health classes.

My husband and I are very comfortable with our bodies around Brooklyn. This is first out of convenience, but also out of a desire to cultivate an appreciation and acceptance of her own human form. She went to every prenatal visit, exams and all.

71

Brooklyn saw me bleed each month prior to pregnancy. I prepared her for what she would hear and see during my labor. I let her nurture me—I encouraged her to nurture me. Every day when I had morning sickness she was there rubbing my back, holding my hair, and telling me it would soon be over. I feel we prepared her thoroughly for not only witnessing, but also being an active member of Shamus's birth. I anticipated being more relaxed during labor, knowing that my little cuddle-bug was within reach.

At one in the morning, I felt my first contractions. I crept downstairs to sleep on the couch. On my way, I heard, "Mommom, what are you doing?"

I told her the baby was getting ready to be born. She wanted to be with me. The two of us slept together until a few hours later, when I felt it was time to make the cookies I wanted to bring to the hospital staff. She slept on and off until around six, when my husband, with his usual good sense, said, "Pam, we need to go, now!"

My little girl was right there from the first contraction until the last. The hospital staff was so pleasant to her, and I think they were amused at having such a little person there for a birth. I remember calling out Brook's name during a tough contraction, and that she and my midwife were discussing Sesame Street.

When I was in transition and really having a time of it, she came into the bathroom and someone thought maybe she shouldn't join me at that moment. I called for her, and she held my hands just like we practiced so many times on the "potty" before. I felt her hands on mine, her hands on my face, as I described in detail every piece of clothing she was wearing. I'll never forget that one contraction, and the peace that she brought to help me cope with it. When it was time to push Shamus out, my husband held her near me, and the two of them encouraged me the whole way. She saw her little brother come out of me. My husband, midwife, and doula so calmly described things to her and to me the whole time. When she realized he was a boy, she told me, "Mama he has a member!" I have never had such a sweet chuckle.

Having Brook at Shamus's birth was one of the wisest decisions I've ever made. I wouldn't have done it without the inspiration of Marjie and Jay Hathaway, founders of the Bradley Method of Natural Childbirth and advocates of siblings at birth. I think it worked so beautifully because we did it responsibly and with love. The discussions, videos, books, office visits, and tours made it comfortable for her. Having a doula made me feel safe, knowing that I would be taken care of in case my husband needed to focus his attention on Brooklyn. I've learned to not underestimate the wonderful nature and beauty of my little girl. I honestly believe that having her there brought a deeper element of unity to our family. She just went with it as if this were something ordinary; she was herself. She wasn't overly sweet, or dramatically worried—only curious and excited.

Now, Brook's behavior during the birth reflects how she handles herself as a sister. She has wholeheartedly accepted Shamus as a member of our family. She doesn't smother him— she is too busy being a three-year-old. She doesn't seem resentful. Only once has she asked me to put him down, when she was sick with a stomach virus. I think she knows that babies need to be attached to their mothers. She embraces sharing story times, cuddle times, and bath times with him. This is something I am so thankful for.

Of course there have been many trying times being the mom of a three-year-old and a newborn. Brooklyn does the usual exasperating things that three-year-olds do. However, no matter how much I feel overwhelmed during the course of a hectic day, at night while she is sleeping, I sneak in for a kiss and silently thank her for being so wonderful at the birth. It's like I can't stay mad at her when I remember how helpful she was to me during my pregnancy and delivery. I feel closer to her for having shared that sacred moment together. This was the first step in our sharing and bonding as women, at the tender age of three. She is my buddy, my little doula, my little daughter who has made all the difference in the world to me.

When someone asks her what she wants to be when she grows up, I laugh when she says "a midwife," and I see the look on their faces. My birth team and I have given my daughter a healthy impression of childbearing and mothering. We still reflect on the birth. She talks about it and her brother with excited chatter. I don't know if Brook will remember Shamus being born in years to come, so I periodically bring the topic up in hopes that she will continue to remember. I like to believe we've built a healthy foundation from which to nurture our family unity. Now continues the responsibility of cultivating their sibling relationship though mindful and compassionate parenting.

❋ ❋ ❋ ❋ ❋

Anyone interested in preparing a sibling for birth may contact me at phrgp@cs.com.

Pamela Fellner *and her husband, Brian, are both twenty-nine and have two children: Shamus, three months, and Brooklyn, three and a half. Both were born naturally, using the principles of the Bradley Method. She currently teaches Bradley Method in Chatham, New Jersey.*

STORY OF CHARLIE'S ARRIVAL
Sally Flanagan

My first baby, Molly, was breech at thirty-five weeks and never turned head down. Because I was naïve, and because I was working with a very traditional OB-GYN, I was not encouraged or offered alternative ways of turning her around. I was simply told that I would need a cesarean section. I was shocked; I had prepared myself to give birth vaginally. But still, I trusted the doctors, and scheduled myself for a C-section reluctantly believing they were right. Needless to say, my story is similar to that of most women who undergo this very disappointing surgery. Pain, sadness, frustration, and longing. I had a terrible reaction to the surgery drugs that included severe nausea for weeks. On top of that, I caught "a nasty intestinal bug" from the hospital, or something else my doctor could never explain. I can still remember those first ten days after her birth, saying to myself, "Next pregnancy, I will have a natural birth no matter what it takes, because nothing can be as painful as this is right now!" And that pain set me on a mission to research vaginal birth after cesarean (VBAC).

I started with Henci Goer's book, *The Thinking Woman's Guide to a Better Birth*. This should be a mandatory read for all mothers-to-be. It is extremely informational and instructional. Next, after many interviews and lengthy discussions with midwives, I decided to start going to a CNM in my area. It was difficult to pick a midwife, because you must use the hospital where they practice. (I wanted the option for a water birth, or at least the choice to labor in the water, but my hospital did not provide that service to mothers.) I decided on a midwife who had a high success rate for VBACs. Tina seemed well-suited to my personality, and assured me that everything would be okay, and that everyone would leave us alone at the hospital during the birth. Therefore, I started working with her well before I got pregnant.

Two years later, we got pregnant with Charlie. From the get-go, we knew he was a big baby, but I would not know how big until many months later. Sean and I were elated. I felt well enough through the beginning, and then I started to really pack on the pounds: twenty, thirty, forty, and then fifty!

I expected this pregnancy to be much the same as my first, but it was very different. Mentally and physically, I was tired from chasing my two-year-old. My patience was diminishing, and I struggled not to complain. (I failed there.) Overall, I just found it hard to be pregnant. It was no longer the glamorous new experience it once was. I loved the life growing inside me, and I loved when it kicked, but I did not have the leisure time to watch my diet and enjoy the growing belly. Sean was my backbone. As always, his positivity overflowed and kept all of us on track through the next ten months, despite my hormonal ups and downs.

For this pregnancy, we signed up for Bradley classes: ten weeks of information about natural birth. These classes were instrumental in the success of our Charlie's birth. (Our doula, Laura, was also the instructor, and so I had the added benefit of knowing that she would be there to support and instruct me through the tough parts of the birthing process.)

I cannot say enough positive things about the Bradley Method. It is so "right on" about so many things. It gives new parents excellent natural guidance for caring for themselves during and after pregnancy, as well tips on newborn children and breastfeeding. It uses a straightforward approach to difficult subjects like circumcision and epidurals. Most importantly, it provides an arena for parents to talk about and reflect upon pregnancy. We were the only ones in the class with a baby already at home, but still, I felt as if I were starting over. Of course, nothing can really prepare you for the experience of labor and birth, but Bradley is the best option out there. It is open-minded in content and honors pregnancy in a beautiful way.

In addition, I took four private sessions of HypnoBirthing. This is, in essence, learning how to relax so deeply that you can actually hypnotize yourself to ease the pain. I ended up not using the method to help me during birth, but it helped me relax before the birth and let go of some the past birth fears. In addition, I loved the teacher, Valerie. During labor, however, for me it was just survival. Instinctual animal reactions kicked in—loud moans, rocking, and breaking blood vessels under my eyes from pushing.

I don't know what I imagined would happen, but I was so curious to find out. It boggled my mind that you wait ten months for a short day of this indescribable event. I guess I really thought that my pain threshold was high, and so I could handle doing it naturally. The truth: it hurt a lot more than I was prepared for. I kept trying to think to myself, "Your body knows what to do." Of course, we had heard so many things about the actual "event" that I was totally confused. What did a contraction really feel like? I didn't know, because I had had a scheduled C-section before. How would I know when to go to the hospital? How was I supposed to push? I must have had more questions and a birth plan with more details and directions than anyone in the history of natural birthing. But my midwife understood my apprehensions and answered all of my questions with sound advice. Tina was incredibly supportive and sweet about my obsessive quest for a satisfying birth the second time around. Sean was right there with me the whole way. He was worried about my pain, but he encouraged me that I could do it if I believed that I could. However, he also told me on numerous occasions that I could change my mind at any moment and it would be no big deal. So that was my plan. Go for it and see what happens. I secretly wanted to do it for Sean, too. I wanted him to see me give birth the way millions of women do all over the world. I wanted to see how strong I was and how determination can bring success. I wanted him to hold me afterwards and be in awe of a woman's body.

Mistake number 201: I had myself convinced that I would go early. My doula warned us that it was dangerous to think that way, and I should consider myself a first-timer since I was a

VBAC. I should have listened. Six weeks before my due date, I was having a lot of contractions—or so I thought. Two weeks before my due date, I was fifty percent effaced. One week before my date, I was ninety percent effaced and two centimeters dilated. I started having the irregular-but-constant contractions on my due date. However, labor would start and stop for the next three days. I was completely frustrated, calling my doula every day, checking in, asking her if this was labor. "No," she said, "not until your contractions are two minutes apart."

Patience was not a virtue I learned during this pregnancy. Anxiety seemed to be my virtue. Three days after my due date passed, I dragged myself into Tina's office for a non-stress test that showed I had had a couple of contractions but was not in active labor. These contractions were painful ones and I was sure I would die in *real* labor. I went home and tried to rest—all the while timing my contractions, another obsession. Later that day, they were occurring within about seven minutes of each other, but then to ten minutes, and back to seven again.

Finally, around 4 p.m., my mother looked at me and said, "If you are that miserable, go the hospital and get induced." I can honestly say she was right about this one. I was scared to call and tell Tina that I wanted to be induced, but I was at my end point. I called and she said that she was expecting our call. We arranged to meet one hour later at labor and delivery. Sometime in that one hour, I must have finally relaxed enough from knowing that it was actually going to happen that my contractions started really coming. I loved the car ride, and remember looking at Sean, thinking, "This babe is soon going to be in our arms." By the time I was hooked up to the monitor, the contractions were two minutes apart. She gave me the smallest bit of Pitocin just to keep them regular. I was glad for that because I wanted this baby out so darn badly.

Those first two hours in the hospital, I went from four centimeters to five centimeters. It seemed like a long time and a lot of hard work for just one centimeter. Then in one hour, I dilated from five centimeters to ten centimeters and was ready to push. I remember learning that transition was the most difficult part. When my doula said I was there, I expected to be throwing up; but really, as much as it hurt, I was still clear. I felt like was watching myself do this from outside my body. Something else takes over inside and goes for it to get that baby out. It was truly an out-of-body experience. I was screaming and moaning. (I was a little embarrassed, in fact. I imagined the entire L and D ward standing outside saying, "We got crazy in there.") I felt best standing up rocking than doing anything else. I just kept thinking to myself, "I can not believe women keep doing this."

After I had resigned myself to the fact that I was going to *die*, I could pretty much endure the pain of my entire lower half spitting up the middle. Sean was adorable. I know he was worried sick, and every once in a while, I would look over at him, but I knew he was in the same place I was: another dimension. Here I was, his wife, in the worst pain imaginable but electing to do this to bring another human into the world. I was so glad he was there. I did not much feel like being touched, so he fed me one ice chip after the other just to occupy my mind.

Laura, my doula, was incredible. She was like the voice of a woman angel who had been there three times before. Right when I needed a word of encouragement, she would whisper the perfect thing to me. "It's okay Sal, labor is hard work and you are doing so well." "It's a big baby and it's almost over, now." I loved knowing that I could get mad at her when it hurt instead of complaining to my husband.

Approaching ten centimeters, things got bad, and I used our "code word" for giving me the epidural. However, no one listened. They all knew how badly I wanted to do this and so, instead, they offered me a muscle relaxant, Nubain. I said fine but quick— I was bursting with pain. They gave me a shot and it felt like ecstasy for all of ten seconds, until the next contraction, and then I felt no relief. Then it was time to push. People say they like pushing, but I thought it was absolute torture. I could hardly pull those legs up and push—was she crazy? But I did, and finally got the knack of it. All the while screaming some morose mantra like, "Oh God—just take me now." And crossing myself. What? I am hardly religious, but this seemed so right at the time that I was constantly crossing myself—Father, Son, and Holy Spirit. An hour and a half later, the head crowned, and I told Tina to cut me. I just knew by the look on their faces this baby wasn't coming out and God, I needed it out at all costs. She did, and then I tore some more. The head coming out felt like a watermelon dropping through the spout of a kitchen sink. *Oh my goodness, that burned.* But then I could touch his head—soft and fuzzy and *alive.* I watched as his huge shoulders slid out, and then, finally, he lay on my stomach. The immediate relief was indescribable. I was surprised at how little blood comes out on the baby. He looked gorgeous.

Sean was set to announce the sex, but a nurse came in at the very last minute (who had not been there the whole time), looked down, and said, "It's a boy." Silence spread across the room, and she looked as if she had just committed a felony. I looked at her and said, "Do not do that." She left the room, ashamed that she had ruined that sacred moment by being stupid. But at that point it didn't matter. Sean couldn't believe it was actually a boy—his *son.* I had told him we were having a boy, but neither of us could believe it was true. I tried to rip away my gown to lay the naked sweet boy on my chest. He wasn't much into the boob at that moment, so we all just sat there for a while, laughing and sighing and saying, "Holy moly—he is *huge.*" And he was: ten pounds, six ounces. I felt so clear, so alive, so incredibly powerful to have just done what I did. I was so very alert. I took some arnica and walked right to the bathroom on my own. I felt like I had just run a marathon but still had energy. This is the difference between drugs and no drugs. Technically, I guess I did have a shot of Nubain and Pitocin to keep the contractions regular, but I was not numb as I would have been with the epidural. I felt everything—every inch of the baby coming into the world. Another great part is saying that I did it. Yeah—I had wanted to do it, and I did. I am not sure I ever really thought I could, but I did it. Birth is one of those amnesic things. You have to really pull everything you have inside to survive it and then just days or weeks later you think you want to do it again. What a bloody trip. I love that it is over, and I can look back with pride. If we were to have another, I would have a natural birth again. After all, there are very few events that are life-changing, and I want to be sober for the magic.

By the way, Charlie is perfect, of course. I never imagined loving a second creature as much as I loved the first. I had forgotten how sweet and sensual the love between a newborn and its momma is. Intoxicating and delicious. Every new thing—just the breath, the breathing, the aroma, and then he smiles. Life is beautiful.

Sally Flanagan writes: *My husband, Sean, and I met in college on Semester at Sea but did not date until later at a friend's wedding. We dated long distance until I moved to New York City. We got pregnant fourteen days after our honeymoon and moved to New Jersey before our first baby girl was born, Molly. Sean is a high school teacher, and I work at home making little books and being a mom to Molly and now, Charlie. I didn't know that I was going feel so attached to the natural way of raising a baby, but I clearly am. It has provided me with a model I feel comfortable with. I never could follow a schedule. I can be reached at Sallyflan@aol.com.*

HOME BIRTH
OR
HOW I OVERCAME STAGE FRIGHT
Talitha Sherman

You may think that home birth and stage fright have nothing to do with each other. I wouldn't have believed it if I hadn't lived it, but giving birth cured me of stage fright. Here's how it happened.

Ever since my first preschool ballet class, I dreamed of becoming a dancer. Though my teachers said I had talent, I was always extremely nervous when performing in front of an audience. I was very critical of my skills and sure that everyone else was better than I was. I loved to dance but was afraid to fail. This performance fear took on new ferocity in my teens when I became so afraid of ridicule and embarrassment that I lost the nerve to dance at all, even in class. The fear won over the joy. It seemed better to protect myself from failure than to risk reaching for my dream.

I hid my hopes away until it became clear that avoidance wasn't helping me overcome my fear and could cost me any chance I had of being a dancer. Not wanting to be haunted by regret, I determined to start taking classes again no matter how scary it was. It took seven years to work up the courage to start again.

Finally, one September day, I took my first belly dancing class. I hated it. After years of letting my skills deteriorate, I was pretty awful. I was so afraid of being put down by my classmates that it was all I could do to make myself stay in the class. I stuck with it, though, having to give myself a little pep talk before each class. My teacher finally kicked me out of the beginning class, insisting I was ready for more advanced technique. I wanted to stay in my comfort zone and not risk more embarrassment. Eventually, she pushed me to accept an invitation to join a belly dance troupe and perform in local venues. Each time I performed in front of an audience, I would shake and feel like running away. I was doing it, but my lack of faith in myself made it extremely hard.

While I was jumping small hurdles in the dance world, my husband graduated from college. We decided that the time was right to start our family. Wanting to give our baby the best beginning, I quit smoking, kicked the caffeine habit, and improved my diet. Combining that with the regular exercise of dancing made us confident that my body was ready and we would soon have the world's most wonderful child in our arms.

That confidence seemed justified when we conceived immediately, but it was shattered three days after taking a positive pregnancy test. I started bleeding and we lost the baby. We were overwhelmed with sadness and doubts. Try not to worry, everyone told us, this happens all the time. We were young and living a healthy life. Next time everything would be perfect.

One month later, pregnant again! Yes, the doctor told us, this pregnancy seemed to be going along just fine. At ten weeks, the spotting started. Then the bad news, no heartbeat. After the trauma of hospitalization and a D and C, we were told it was safe to try again.

Only now, we were really worried. Nothing else seemed very important anymore, not even the dancing I had devoted so much of myself to. What if we never had a child of our own? What if I never had the experience of carrying and giving birth to my own baby? I had done everything right! I knew women who never gave a thought to what they put into their bodies, and they had children. Why not me?

Two months later, no period.

Feeling unsure of my body's capability to successfully complete this pregnancy, I knew my doctor would have to be the best. During the miscarriages, my doctors were very patronizing and didn't understand how shaken I was. They also had not been able to detect any problems with my pregnancies, or save my babies. The doctor with whom I gave birth would have to treat me better.

After calling every doctor in town, I chose the one that seemed the best. Unfortunately, my new doctor was even less supportive. She didn't make eye contact once, mispronounced my name, and completely ignored my husband. Our previous losses didn't seem to matter to her at all. But we had a heartbeat! Oh well, I thought, maybe she'll grow on me. Maybe it doesn't matter if the person who witnessed the greatest day of my life is a cold fish. Maybe I'll get used to being treated like a number, and it will stop making me feel small and unimportant.

My husband and I were so excited about the baby that we toured the hospital before I was even showing. The hospital was as bad as the doctor was: cold, impersonal and mechanized. Oh well, I thought, maybe it will grow on me. Maybe I'll get used to the idea of not being able to have my family with me. Maybe I'll get comfortable with the idea of a complete stranger touching me and deciding whether or not to cut me. Maybe I'll get over being forced to let my baby leave with nurses I've never met before. But I didn't get over it. Instead, I had nightmares.

"What about home birth?" my husband said. He had suggested it before and I had told him in no uncertain terms that he was crazy. Babies died in childbirth! Women died in childbirth! And there were no pain-relief drugs at home! Of course, we had lost two babies under a doctor's care and in a hospital. So I started reading and was surprised to learn that home birth is actually safer than hospital birth. I decided that maybe my husband was not so crazy. But would my body work right? Could I do it without drugs?

Deciding to at least investigate our options, we began the search for a midwife who attended home births. We found only one. I was still not convinced, but I went to meet with her. Little did I know that I was on my way to meet a woman who would prove to be one of the most positive influences in my life. She answered all my questions and made me realize for the first time that maybe I could do this. She seemed so strong and had confidence in my ability to birth naturally. "What you need," she told me, "is to take Bradley classes." She put me in touch with a teacher, and in no time at all, my husband and I were sitting in a room full of round ladies who, with me, were learning to trust their bodies.

As my tummy grew and we looked forward to our baby's arrival, I found I was struggling with performance anxiety about the birth itself. I would be in front of an audience again and this time, horror of horrors, I would be naked! People might even see me do things I would normally only do in the privacy of my bathroom. Maybe they would see me get mean or panic. Maybe I would lose control. Maybe they would be disappointed with me. Maybe I would fail.

Well, the big day arrived and lo and behold, I did lose control. My body did do things I usually keep private. My family did see me naked. To my complete surprise, not only did they not tease or put me down, they were in awe of me! They told me over and over how amazing I was. My mom said she had never seen anything so wonderful in her life, and she's a doctor! My stepfather was so touched and honored to attend the birth that he, big strong man, cried. My mother-in-law said witnessing a new life coming into the world in such a loving way renewed her faith in God. Wow! If I was able to go through all that pain, exposure, and risk, be a part of such an extraordinary event, and gain the admiration of others, then I could certainly do something as simple as dancing in front of people. What if they didn't like my performance? So what? I gave birth to my child in my home and did it beautifully! On that glorious day, my child was born into the world, but I was born into my own power. For the rest of my life I will dance for pure joy with nothing left to prove.

Talitha Sherman *is now the mother of three beautiful home-born, breastfed daughters, Kira, Sadie, and Hazel. Hoping to help other couples have beautiful, transformational births, she and her husband Daniel teach the Bradley Method of Natural Childbirth. A La Leche League Leader for three years, she holds monthly meetings for mothers interested in breastfeeding. If you visit Southern California, you can find her performing and teaching belly dancing, stretch marks and all.*

FINDING MY WAY HOME
ONE MOTHER'S JOURNEY FROM
HOSPITAL C-SEC TO HOME VBAC

Rachel Gathercole

I have never considered myself an Earth Mother. A modern woman, degreed and career-bound, I never even thought I'd stay home with my kids. I certainly never imagined I would have a home birth. At least, not when I first became a mom. All I wanted was a safe birth and a healthy baby. In fact, when my first child was born, by cesarean section, I had never even heard of home birth, let alone considered it. If I had heard of it, I probably would have thought it sounded nuts.

Besides, I was going to have a natural birth in the hospital (only the best for my baby!) and everything would be peachy. Why wouldn't it be? I had lined up the best obstetrician and hospital in town, I had good insurance, I took childbirth classes at the hospital, and I practiced my breathing. That was what it was all about, right? Just for good measure, and to be sure I communicated my plans clearly so the helpful hospital staff would know I wanted an unmedicated, noninterventionist birth, I wrote up a birth plan. I was sure this would give my baby and me every advantage toward having the best and *safest* birth possible. How could I know that the safest birth of all lay not in the hospital, but in the most unexpected of places?

As it turned out, none of the staff at that hospital were interested in my ideas or aspirations about natural birth. My birth plan was not graced with a single glance from my doctor or any of the hospital staff. They had their own plan—the one they always followed with every laboring mother: standard operating procedure. They would get on with it and move me along just like everybody else.

So I received, almost immediately upon arrival, the hospital's routine interventions: enema, catheter, IV, internal monitor, epidural, and finally, a cesarean section (which is widely documented in the medical literature as a risk of all of the above "routine" procedures). This was not an "emergency" cesarean; no medical problems were documented, or existed, with me or the baby. It was just another intervention. But it was a big one.

Immediately after the surgery, I was separated from my healthy baby for many hours and suffered pain, exhaustion, engorgement, breastfeeding difficulties, and postpartum depression. My baby received artificial feeding without my consent, and as a result, had jaundice and nipple confusion. On the first night of his life, starting just moments after his birth, he cried all night, alone, without my knowledge.

Everything was not peachy.

In the years that followed, I became a more informed mom, reading and talking to more experienced mothers about breastfeeding, discipline, healthcare, and yes, birth. I discovered firsthand, through breastfeeding and nurturing my son naturally, what amazing things my body could do on its own. And at the same time, I began to find things out. First by accident, through the stories of other mothers' experiences. Then by further research.

Home birth, I was surprised to discover, is actually quite safe. In fact, outcomes and statistics for home birth compare favorably to hospital birth. Scientific research shows that home birth boasts lower perinatal mortality and morbidity rates at all levels of risk than hospital birth, and home birth results in lower rates of infection and intervention, including cesarean section. And not only is it safe, I learned, but it has many advantages over hospital birth: convenience (no rushing around), freedom (no schedules to adhere to, beds to be confined to, etc.), biological familiarity (no unfamiliar bacteria to cause infection), family togetherness (no separation from loved ones), and more.

After a great deal of research, I knew that there was no reason that I, even as a VBAC (vaginal birth after cesarean), couldn't birth at home, and every reason that I should.

So when I was pregnant with my second child, I had different plans. Thanks to a few great books and some wonderful women I met in a breastfeeding support group, I had become informed and empowered about birth. I planned to have a VBAC, and knew now that home could offer the kind of birth I wanted.

I sought out and found a great lay midwife. She was more than competent and very supportive of my plans. During our regular, hour-long visits, we discussed at length all aspects of my pregnancy and upcoming birth. When the day came for me to labor, it was just as I had hoped. Home birth may not be for everyone, but for me it was "just what the midwife ordered."

There was no panic, no bright lights, no unnecessary interventions of any kind. Just labor and support. Using yoga techniques I had practiced at my midwife's suggestion during pregnancy, I labored in the comfort of my home, supported and safe, while my midwife, labor assistant, and husband helped me through every contraction. They used massage, effleurage (touch), soothing words, breathing guidance, and warm water to ease my pain and keep me focused. There were many occasions on which I was distinctly aware that being here, at home with my midwife, was very likely enabling me to avoid having a repeat cesarean section, because the midwife had up her sleeve an effective noninterventionist solution or approach to every issue that came up. She knew how to avoid and address simple, natural events in labor that in the hospital would certainly have been met with risky interventions. Yes, it was difficult. It was labor. But it was the way I wanted it to be—natural and safe. And it was all worth it when finally, in a birth tub in my living room, I pushed out a beautiful, chubby, rosy, ten-and-a-quarter-pound baby girl!

At once tired and exhilarated, I sat in the tub, holding her close in this womb-like setting that enclosed us both. After a while, I climbed out and sat on the couch, where she suckled peacefully at my breast, and I chatted and laughed with my husband and birth attendants. Eventually they took some time to tend to postpartum matters: cleaning up and, of course, weigh-ing, checking, and diapering the baby. Then, when we all felt ready, the midwife and her helpers said goodnight, promising to return in the morning, and left. I, the happy "new" mother, snuggled up in bed with my husband, son, and perfect little baby, and went to sleep.

No jaundice, no separation, no depression, no engorgement, no exhaustion. Just a new baby, an enamored brother, and a tired mom and dad snoring together and recovering from a long day's truly hard work. In the morning we awoke happy, healthy, nurs-ing, and full of surprising energy—a new-and-improved family of four.

"Peachy" doesn't even begin to describe it.

Of course, mine is only one of many happy home-birth stories. As the good news about home birth's great outcomes and count-less benefits becomes better known, this birth option is becom-ing more and more popular. People are starting to realize that home birth really is a practical, sensible choice. And naturally, not all families come to this decision by the same route I did.

In fact, people choose home birth for a variety of reasons, including any or all of the following: safety, comfort, conven-ience, family togetherness, control, avoidance of unnecessary intervention, reduced risk of cesarean section, desire for a com-petent, noninterventionist, supportive birth attendant, lower cost, and/or religious or spiritual reasons. There are many others as well.

The magic of home birth is that no matter what your reason for choosing it, you get all of these many rewards in the package.

And what a beautiful package it is!

For more information on home birth and VBAC, please see the following great books:

Bean, Constance. *Methods of Childbirth.*

Cohen, Nancy and Lois J. Estner. *Silent Knife: Cesarean Prevention and Vaginal Birth After Cesarean.*

Gaskin, Ina May. *Spiritual Midwifery.*

Korte, Diana and Roberta Scaer. *A Good Birth, A Safe Birth.*

Sears, William and Martha. *The Birth Book.*

Stewart, David. *The Five Standards for Safe Childbearing.*

Rachel Gathercole *is a freelance writer and the breastfeeding, co-sleeping, sling-wearing, home-birthing, home-schooling mother of two children, ages eight and four. Her articles and essays on motherhood, children, and related topics have appeared in numerous national and local publications. She resides with her husband and children in North Carolina, where she continues to make her way on the incredible journey of motherhood.*

The Planned Home Birth but Unplanned, Unassisted Birth of Saumaya Charles Schneider, April 11, 2002

Gwen Charles

Sunday morning, April 7

Slept terrible. I woke up frantic. Major nesting urges. I *needed* to get everything done that was not done yet. I still didn't have curtains for the living room where I planned on giving birth, the birthing pool was not set up, the diaper changing table was not set up, the bedroom needed to be rearranged. I pushed my husband to do as much as he could before going to work, which was difficult since our son wanted to play. My husband could see that I was anxious and scolded me for the look I had in my eye. Do not move any furniture, he told me before leaving. My mom took me shopping for curtains and nursing nightgowns. I went to sleep feeling that we got a few more things done.

❋ ❋ ❋ ❋ ❋

Monday morning, 3 a.m.

I woke up to go to the bathroom and was surprised to see blood. "Show," they call it. My midwife had mentioned that show usually means labor will begin in twenty-four to forty-eight hours. I went downstairs to tell Gary working in the studio; he heard my footsteps and came to the stairs. He asked me what was up—I told him and started to shake all over.

"What's the matter?"

"I'm nervous."

93

"About what? You're a pro at this."

I started to cry. I listed all the things I was worried about: worried that I couldn't be as good a parent as I was for Guito, nervous that two children will be overwhelming, etc. etc. Gary was calm and held me. He told me that we were good parents, he mentioned that there are many people in the world with more than one child, etc. etc. I felt better just to have said all my fears out loud. I announced several times, "I am ready. I am ready. I am ready for this baby."

Monday morning

I woke up hoping that I could get everything else done today. But instead I was disappointed to realize that once I got out of bed, I would get nothing done. I was dizzy and sluggish. I had no appetite. I felt like that old V-8 commercial where everyone is walking crooked. I still saw show and called the midwife to let her know. Cara said twenty-four to seventy-two hours now. I called my mother to see if she could come over the next day so I could rest. She couldn't. I took a short nap. Our neighbor called and said, "Come over." I needed a distraction, so we spent the day looking for a hamper for her home. I was glad not to be at home today.

We went to bed early.

Tuesday morning

I woke up after sleeping over ten hours. I felt relaxed. A calmness had swept over my body. Everything had slowed down. I felt soft, warm, and cozy inside. I was no longer concerned with rushing to finish anything. I hoped I could sustain that calmness until and throughout the labor. I could not move very quickly, so I decided to cancel my appointments planned in the city the next day. My husband took the day off. He built the birth pool we rented (our son was born at home in the tub in our last apartment, but this house has only a shower stall), got the diaper table from the attic, put the futon cover on, and neatened up the house. We felt ready. I went to sleep early. The night was quiet and the baby did not move much, a sign that labor was very near.

* * * * *

Wednesday

I had slept over ten hours again. I felt great and well-rested, and the calmness continued. Our friends came over, and we went for a walk into town. The children rode their bikes. Mothers waiting to pick up their children at the school across the street looked at me as if I shouldn't have been allowed out. It was a beautiful, sunny, warm day, and we played outside all afternoon. I was feeling so good and was starving after hardly eating for two days. We ate dinner in their yard and walked home happy that we spent a wonderful day together. Guito and I were exhausted, and we went to sleep early, around 9 p.m.

I woke up at 1:44 a.m. Thursday morning, April 11, with a feeling low in the front of my pelvis. The baby was descending. I wasn't sure if it was a contraction. I decided to count how long it lasted, just in case. I waited to see if I would feel another. Five minutes later a stronger feeling in the low of my back, definitely a contraction, began. I watched the clock—digital, so I knew it was about a minute long. I got up out of bed to tell Gary; he was working downstairs in the studio. He heard my footsteps and started to come up and asked if I was okay. I told him to go to bed soon since the baby would be here tomorrow afternoon. He was excited to hear it and went to finish up his work. I went back upstairs expecting to go back to bed.

About five minutes later, another contraction began. The contraction was strong, and I felt like I needed comfort. I felt alone, with no one there to hold me. I wondered if maybe I should call some family and friends to come over and stay with me. I imagined a room full of people I loved telling me stories and rubbing my back, letting me know that I am supported. I went back downstairs.

"Gary, I think you should start counting these."

I told him that I needed some comfort and that I didn't know what to do. He came upstairs. Then, the night changed. The next contraction came on strong, deep within my back—I had to hold on to the wall. I grunted and felt a huge urge to push. Gary asked if I could speak through it—I couldn't. Gary called the midwife, called his mom in the next town over. (She was a childbirth educator, La Leche League Leader, also a home birth mom.) The midwife said she would come right away—it would be about an hour. Gary's mother didn't answer the phone and he left a message. He went to get the hose to fill up the birthing pool. When the contraction ended, I went to sit on the toilet. Maybe I just needed to go to the bathroom. I was trying to deceive myself. I did not want to believe that I could have the urge to push this baby out yet. The midwife was at least an hour away, and I hadn't had any earlier signs of labor. Where was the beginning? Where was the transition period? How could I have been all the way at the end of labor? Wouldn't I tear, pushing this hard, so fast? Where was Gary's mom? I asked him to please call her again. This time she answered, and she was on her way.

I was just going to the bathroom, I told myself. Big mistake to sit on the toilet. In this semi-squatting position, my hips and pelvis opened—the night moved on quickly. I no longer thought of being comforted. My body took over. A huge contraction began, causing pressure from my lower back and giving me a strong urge to push. I gave a loud grunt like a goose honking; my water broke, and I felt the head crowning.

Gary came into the bathroom and heard me, and started to panic. "Stop. Hold it. Don't push, don't push. You didn't push Guito for hours, remember? You can hold this one."

"I can't. It's coming."

Gary's face changed. He became serious, and I think he was ready now for reality: we were going to deliver this baby ourselves.

"Well then, you have to get off the toilet. I can't catch a baby like that."

I didn't want to get off the toilet—I was comfortable there, but he was right—there was no one else who could catch the baby if he was going to hold me up. I decided to get on all fours.

I hoped that I could slow the labor this way, and prevent a tear. Gary threw down two brown towels on the bathroom floor and I got down on them. I heard, "Oh my god, there's the head."

I wanted to laugh; did he think I was joking? But another contraction began. Gary grabbed the first oil he could find in the bathroom—Arnica oil (for sore muscles) and rubbed it around the perineum. The baby's head was delivered.

I felt comfort wash over me to feel that this was working. Gary held the head. Time stopped for a moment—it felt as if the space between the end of the last contraction and the beginning of the next was longer than any other. Gary asked if I was okay, and I asked if he was okay, and we both said yes. The next contraction came, and I said, "Here we go." Gary held each body part as it came out. His breathing got heavy and loud, and he said, "Oh," with each body part. I could feel the body slither out and liquid pour out of my body. I sighed a sigh of relief.

The phone started to ring, and we knew it must be the midwife, Cara.

He told me it was a girl, and that I should turn over and hold her so he could get the phone. I could not think of moving. Then, somehow, Gary helped me flip over, umbilical cord still connected, and I sat down on the wet floor. He handed me the baby and grabbed a towel to cover her.

He answered the phone—when he told the midwife it was a girl, she laughed and said, "Yeah, right." Gary said, "No really, it's a girl." She asked a range of questions to see how everything was.

I was looking at my baby. Her eyes were closed, and she started to cry. Guito was sleeping in the next room, woke suddenly, and gave out a tremendous fearful yell: "*Dad!*" Gary threw the cordless headset phone on my head and went running to comfort Guito. As soon as he told him it was the baby, Guito got quiet and wanted to go see. When he saw her and heard her cry, he giggled. We realized that the light was too bright for her, so Gary threw a towel over the light, and she opened her eyes to see us all.

He helped me up onto the toilet. It was about two thirty, and by now, Gary's mom had arrived and began to help us out. She got a dry towel for the baby, covered the couch with disposable towels, and helped me to move to the living room. The midwife told us via cell phone to hold the placenta, wait to deliver it, and cut the cord while we waited for her to get there. We lay pretty comfortably on the couch (aside from the fact that there was a cold telephone cord coming out of my body). When Cara arrived, she checked us all out, helped deliver the placenta, and checked it. We put it into a Tupperware container and into the freezer for the day when we would finally have a home of our own, and could bury it in the yard. (Tradition in some countries. And yes, if you are curious, we do have Guito's in the freezer, still.) She weighed and checked the baby, then wrapped her in towels warmed in the oven.

I went to take a shower, and Cara's assistant stayed with me. Cara filled out paperwork with all the information about the birth and asked us what time the baby was born. We didn't know. Gary's mom offered the time that she arrived, so we estimated a few minutes before. We also checked the midwife's cell phone call record to see when she called us, and we all settled on 2:26 a.m. The midwife and assistant helped us to clean up and went back to the birth they were attending downtown. Gary rushed downstairs to send a frantic e-mail to friends and family about the amazing night. I went to bed with the new baby on one side and my son on the other. My adrenaline was still pumping, and I could not sleep. I just lay there thinking about how beautiful my life was.

✳ ✳ ✳ ✳ ✳

To read about water birth, go to:
www.waterbirth.org.

To read about home birth, go to:
www.midwiferytoday.com/articles/homebirthchoice.asp.

Gwen Charles is a visual artist and art educator. Both of her children were born at home. Gwen has combined her art background and interest in natural parenting in her breastfeeding clothing business, www.umamawear.com.

THE VALUE AND PURPOSE OF LABOR SUPPORT

Jill Gerken Wodnick

Throughout history, females have faced difficulty in making their voices heard publicly. For years, society has classified women as being the inferior gender. As Karyln Kohrs Campbell states in her book, *Man Cannot Speak For Her*, "Men have an ancient and honorable rhetorical history. Their speeches and writings, from antiquity to present are studied and analyzed by historians and rhetoricians...Women have no parallel rhetorical history. Indeed, for much of their history, women have been prohibited from speaking, a prohibition reinforced by such powerful cultural authorities as Homer, Aristotle, and Scripture..." (1989).

So, without this rhetorical history, women's stories have been told in other ways: through attendance and participation at fertility rites, menarche celebrations, and childbirth. Thus, women supporting other women in labor and birth is important to recall and support in the canon of our history. Anita Diamant's bestselling novel of early midwives and doulas, *The Red Tent*, captures the voice of childbearing women, and served as an inspiration to me during my pregnancy and as I studied to become a doula myself. In the beginning, Dinah (the main character) tells us, "We have been lost to each other for so long. My name means nothing to you. My memory is dust. This is not your fault, or mine. The chain connecting mother to daughter was broken and the word passed to the keeping of men, who had no way of knowing. That is why I became a footnote...." Her fictional history becomes our history as women, a reminder of the voices we no longer hear.

A doula can help women in hearing, crafting, and telling their birth stories. In doing so, doulas offer powerful emotional support before, during, and after labor and birth, as well as pragmatic advice. As a first-time mom, Jennifer in New Jersey shared, "After my baby was born, my mother and sisters did not want to hear my birth story...they just wanted to know the 'statistics' of how many hours I was in labor. They wanted to know the outcome of the baby—not the beginning, middle, and birth of Daniel's story." Our culture codifies birth as a medical, data-based experience; this linear model goes against the organic flow and multisensory experience that labor and birth actually are. As Farley and Widmann explain in their essay on storytelling and birth, "Telling birth stories allows the woman to organize her memories of this life-altering event, to integrate her feelings about the event, and to shape the perceptions of other women who have yet to give birth" (1998).

The emotional support a doula provides has a direct connection to the medical benefits of the service. Doula support has been shown to reduce the need for analgesics, reduce the use of forceps, reduce the length of labor for first-time moms, and increase the woman's satisfaction with her birth experience. Because a doula has a relationship with the family before, during, and after the baby's birth, a doula can provide resources, referrals, and information to assist in going from couple to family; dealing with in-laws; newborn-mother bonding; breastfeeding support and referrals; and reframing, listening, and participating in the mother's birth story. In addition, five research studies using randomized trials have evaluated the impact of a doula in reducing the stress of a modern birth environment.

The purpose behind providing labor support comes from the evidence regarding labor itself: women can receive pain-coping techniques, emotional support, and encouragement if they are not alone. When a woman is encouraged to deeply moan through each contraction, loosening her throat and melting her body, birth takes on an experience that is not just medical, but becomes a transformative rite of passage. Women are heard in labor and their emotional, physical, and sometimes even spiritual needs can be enhanced by a doula's work.

Thus, doulas provide the missing link in women's rhetorical history. Farley and Widmann continue, "Listening to a woman share the birth stories that shape her beliefs about childbearing and childrearing provides insight into her needs at a psychological, spiritual, and emotional level...The understanding gained through listening informs care practices: it promotes sensitive and individualized service through the development of a therapeutic relationship between a woman and her caregiver" (1998).

A doula's job is to provide "high quality labor support to clients as an effective means to improving maternal and child health" (DONA). Clearly, a doula has professional responsibilities that extend beyond listening; but that part of the doula's role cannot be underestimated. To listen is to allow a woman to be heard; it is the essential first step, not only in preparing a successful and healthy birth, but also in remembering a happy birth story—and to be heard and remembered is to be reintroduced to a legacy and way of living that seems almost forgotten in this technological, medical era.

Women supporting other women in labor and birth rarely make history or headlines. Yet, the compassionate words, tender touches, and emotional support that a doula provides is as an important an event during each birth as is an international summit, or as a volcano erupting. One birth at a time, doulas help the transformation of maiden into mother and assist in making birth a rite of passage.

Jill Gerken Wodnick *is an orator, storyteller, mother, wife, certified doula, and Birthing From Within mentor. She is most inspired by texts like "The Artist's Way" and "The Power of Myth." Jill can be found composing essays, singing, and teaching in Bloomfield, New Jersey. Please visit her website: www.WiseWomanBirthways.com.*

POSTPARTUM DEPRESSION AND THE ATTACHED MOTHER

Amy Ekblad

November 11, 2002—It was my oldest daughter's sixth birthday. I went for a routine appointment with my midwife and found out that my fifth baby was breech. No big deal, I thought, he'll turn around. I was only thirty-seven weeks at that point. My midwife wasn't so sure, and scheduled me to have the baby turned, a procedure that was "uncomfortable but not painful," in her words. I got a little nervous when she said it could put me into labor. We planned it for the following Friday, four days away.

The week passed, but slowly. I worried about the baby. I called my doula, who suggested several positions to sit, stand, or lie in. I moved a flashlight around my belly at night, trying to get the baby to follow it. I felt guilty for rushing through this pregnancy, and for not having prepared well enough. After having four babies, I thought it was old hat. What would I have needed besides a few T-shirts, some cloth diapers, and a sling? I hadn't really talked to the baby. Not like I had to the others. I loved him, yes, but I hadn't bonded with him yet. He didn't even have a name. Actually, he had several; we couldn't decide what it should be. I had a number of days picked out that wouldn't be good for him to be born on. Not on Wednesday; it was our busiest day. Dance, guitar, Kindermusik. Not on Thanksgiving. Possibly the day after. Not on December 2; we had plans. Poor baby. I didn't give him much to choose from.

So I sat in a chair in my room thinking about all of this and feeling horribly guilty. I had read that sometimes babies who feel

ignored are breech. It gets them the attention they deserve. I
wondered if that was what my little guy was doing.

The weather turned colder, and I solemnly packed a bag for
the hospital. The day had come for the big turning. I couldn't
sleep the night before. What if they hurt him? I woke up several
times thinking that he was dead inside of me. I screamed to my
husband. I poked my belly, and eventually the baby poked back.
He was fine. I did the Rosary over and over again. We went to
the hospital and waited for hours. Finally, they did an ultrasound
and found that he had turned on his own! All was well.

✳ ✳ ✳ ✳ ✳

November 18—I went for another routine visit to the midwife.
Again the baby was breech. Again they scheduled to turn him on
Friday. Again he was head down.

✳ ✳ ✳ ✳ ✳

November 25—Another routine visit. Another breech baby. This
baby was a gymnast, a swimmer, something special!

✳ ✳ ✳ ✳ ✳

November 26—Baby was still breech. I signed some forms. They
tried to turn him. I squeezed my rosary and cried and screamed.
My husband and mother were there to support me. The procedure was very painful. It was also unsuccessful. They scheduled a
C-section and sent me home. As I sat on the table, I talked to the
baby. "Please turn," I said.

Miraculously, he did.

The hospital staff immediately induced me—another thing I
really didn't want to do. At that point, I was so traumatized that
I called the doula and canceled. I felt like I couldn't face anyone
after allowing so many interventions.

My longest labor thus far had been eight hours. I was sure he
would be born in less.

Nineteen hours and two failed epidurals later, he was born. November 27, 2002. Nameless, he came into the world with his cord wrapped around his neck and in his fist. I feared that he was dead. He was blue. He breathed, slightly. Then, the cry that we all waited to hear.

The next few days grew steadily worse. I couldn't sit up because I had a spinal headache. I also got an infection. I missed Thanksgiving with my four older children. I couldn't take care of the baby. It was all I could do to lie there and nurse. I missed his first bath. I finally went home, but to my parents' house, because I didn't feel confident that I could do this alone.

I spent the next two months in misery, fighting off fears of death, horrible bouts of anxiety, and guilt over this "botched" labor and delivery. I had been anti-meds, anti-intervention, but when push came to shove, I had caved. I lay awake at night fearing that my baby lying next to me was dead. Was he breathing? I couldn't tell. The fear ran so deep. I couldn't enjoy my other children. I was miserable.

Finally, one day, I picked up the phone to make my baby's two-month checkup with the doctor. Almost as an afterthought, I asked if there was a homeopathic remedy for postpartum depression. I went in the next day and was put on an antidepressant. I worried about nursing with it, but the doctor insisted that it was okay. I felt better almost immediately.

That was six months ago. I still struggle sometimes. I still feel guilty about the labor and delivery, and wonder if I did the right thing. I bonded with my baby, though; he's wonderful and healthy. His name is Jackson Andrew.

Amy Ekblad is a stay-at-home, home-schooling, attachment-parenting mom to Brandon, eleven, Hannah, six, Owen, five, Katie, two, and their swimmer Baby Jackson, eight months old. Wife to Jesse. She lives in Canton, Michigan.

SOME CHOICES JUST MAKE THEMSELVES

Barbara Rivera

Sometimes in the choices we make there are no choices at all. Deciding to have our child at home was one of those choices that made themselves.

When I was little, our house was filled with many animals, and as a result, I was lucky to watch dozens of kittens and puppies being born. I anxiously hovered over many laboring cats and dogs wondering how to help, but my mother would tell me every time, "Leave her alone, Barbara, the mother knows what to do," and she was right. Always, the babies would be born, and we would end up with an exhausted but blissful mother curled around a pile of mewling babies.

Birth looked hard, but it seemed worth it. I loved these animal babies, and I wanted to have a baby of my own someday. Anytime there was a new mother and baby around, I would hover around the kitchen and listen as these women talked about their birth with my mother. I was shocked when I heard about how human babies were born; women were expected to get an enema, have their private area shaved, and then spread their legs on a table while a doctor cut the baby out with an episiotomy. I felt humiliated for myself and for all women. After seeing so many amazing animal births, I was revolted by the weak human condition. What happened, I wondered, that humans had become incapable of delivering their babies in a natural way?

The times when I visited the hospital to see friends or family who had given birth, I was troubled as I watched the efficient nurses walk past the rows of crying babies in the nursery. This felt wrong to me, but everyone else acted as if it were all right. I often thought that everyone was crazy. Mothers belonged with their babies.

When I found out that I was pregnant, my disgust with traditional birth options grew. My husband and I toured a local hospital's maternity ward, and I saw that nothing had changed since I was a child. A group of happily expectant parents did not even blink when I asked the nurse to approximate what the cesarean rate was for the hospital. "Just a little over thirty percent" we were told. When I challenged the hospital's mandatory four-hour separation from the baby, other couples sat docilely as I questioned each reason for taking the baby away after the birth. No one seemed concerned or interested about what happened for those hours when the baby was taken to the nursery. As we left the hospital, my husband and I were troubled.

"Why do they need to take the baby away for four hours?" I asked my doctor.

The reply was, "Well, they need to do some procedures, as well as bathe and then warm the baby."

I asked if the hospital could change this policy so I could keep my baby with me, and I was dismissed with a laugh. "Mothers are only too happy to get a rest after the birth, and I am sure you will be, too."

I couldn't imagine that after waiting for nine months, I would be happy to be without my child. The more I asked questions, the more suspicious I felt about what would come once I was helpless in the hospital's care. Little things that were said by my "compassionate doctor" set alarms off inside my head. What really rattled me were statements like, "You are not going to write a birth plan, are you? I find that women who do that are usually in for a big disappointment." As I watched my doctor closely, I could see that under his comforting and placating behavior was his knowledge that once my labor entered the hospital, I would be at the mercy of the "system," and he would do just what he had been trained to do; medicate and interfere with the natural birth process. The more my husband and I learned about the unnecessary procedures, tests, and tortures that our baby would have to go through once he was born, the more we realized that a hospital birth was not for us. To create a more gentle beginning for our baby, we would have to look for an alternative.

After touring the only real birthing center offered in my area, my husband and I had the same concerns: that the drive was too far from our apartment, and that the rooms were very small. Someone suggested a home birth and referred me to Sheila Kitzinger's books on natural birth. I was hooked, and I devoured more books on natural birth. My husband was supportive; his mother had birthed seven out of eight children at home, and he felt that since I was the one giving birth, I had to follow my own instincts about where I felt safe.

Once I made my decision, I spoke powerfully about my birth, even in the face of others' hostility and fear. Family and friends would say things like, "Aren't you afraid to birth at home?" or "If anything goes wrong, it is your fault." And one of the worst, in the guise of "support" for my decision to home birth, came from my mother: "You are selfish to have this baby at home!" To all I replied, "This baby is going to slip right out!" and to my mom, "I am not going to discuss birth with you anymore unless you educate yourself on this issue."

I found my midwife, Mary, through interviewing other midwives and doulas for my birth. Mary seemed to be the midwife most revered by all, and she was the attendant that many chose for their own births. Several conversations with her by telephone and one meeting later, I realized why others spoke of Mary with respect and awe. Mary was the incarnation of "woman power": confident, smart, caring, attentive, and fully present. She was passionately in love with her life's work and with life itself. In her presence, I knew that I could give myself over to the birth process and trust her call if it turned out that I needed to be transferred to the hospital. I knew that I would have no regrets with Mary on my team.

Leandros was born at home after only five hours of active labor and six contractions. As predicted, and with a little bit of help from Mary, he slipped right out! Like the mother cat, I knew what my body wanted to do. Stand up, lean on walls, on all fours in the birthing tub: this was all just a part of the dance to position my baby for the birth. My pain told me where I should be.

I pushed while kneeling, my shoulder on my doula's knee, and the other shoulder on my husband's knee. The final push was done semi-standing, hanging off of my husband, and using him to bear down. Leandros yelled once as he came out and was immediately laid on my belly. He did not cry, but seemed to relax on my stomach while Milton and I greeted him.

Leandros was never taken from us and put in an incubator. He was never suctioned, or stuck with needles, or had burning medicine put into his eyes. He was kept warm as nature intended: his skin on my skin, nestled between my breasts. Later I was told that Leandros had been "sunny side up," and that I had birthed him through the dreaded "back labor." I was thrilled. If I have been in the hospital, this type of labor would have been unbearable if I was forced to labor and deliver on my back.

Did I make a choice to have a home birth? Sure, but when presented with the alternatives, the decision to have a home birth was no choice at all. Each choice made itself because the alternatives were unbearable. I took charge of my birth, choosing the birth attendants and choosing where and how I wanted to labor. My body-wisdom chose how and where my baby was born. Looking back, I mourn for myself as a child and a young lady— and I spent years disgusted with myself as a woman. As I learned about birth, my body seemed to be useless, weak, and comical. If I had known in the past what I know now about the power and the raw beauty of birth, I would have loved being a woman a long time ago. Where will I have my next birth? That will be no choice at all.

Barbara Rivera *does many things as the mother of Leandros and wife to Milton. She is most active in changing diapers, giving baths, singing songs, reciting "Goodnight Moon," doing dishes, and taking long walks. Presently, they are searching for some land in the Catskill Mountains where they can offer a sacred space for spiritual teachings and retreats.*

AND THEN THERE WERE THREE
(A LETTER TO MY FIRSTBORN)
Abigail Dotson

Dear Ruby:

I thought I would write this letter so long ago, before you smiled and stood and learned to look up and utter "mama"; before you took off running, or at least fast-walking; before you pointed at kitties and picked up sticks to shove in the neighbor's dog's mouth, hoping for a game of fetch. This was a story I held in my thoughts before you ever found your sense of humor and learned to joke with me, playing peek-a-boo behind the telephone pole at the park or draping necklaces around my nipples, then laughing at your own silliness; before I heard your boisterous, "Ha-Ha!" or coy, "Tee-hee," your foreboding, "Hot, hot," or your sing-songy, "Heeeeeere, Kitty." (Pronounced "Heeeeeeeehhhh, klllthsscchhhheeeee.") I thought I would tell you this story while you were still a jellybean in my arms, poking your nose into my breast as if to say, "Mama, I wanna nipple." It is a story of an evening that faded into night, and then a night that dawned into a day that so many people will never forget. It is the story of how you came into my arms, my love, and how I got to hold you for the very first time.

I wasn't one of those women who walk around pregnant for months, waiting for people to notice. I never got a chance to be impatient for my belly to swell with the obvious satellite of child inside. Nope, almost as fast as I knew, everybody else did, too. You never were a shy soul, and I suppose that's why you weren't afraid to announce your upcoming arrival from almost the minute your daddy's little sperm swam through the castle walls and found a mate. We used to call you Li'l Kicker for the way you

111

shadowboxed inside me. We would lie together on the couch, your papa, yourself, and me, and he would beat the baby drum in time to his favorite songs. And sometimes you would beat back.

And this is how we danced through our days together, for so many months. And as the days edged on and my hands began to know your bundled up form so well, I started to wonder about the unbundled you. By the time winter rolled around, I stopped thinking the waddle was cute. Each time I heaved my middle-heavy self up, a big round belly on hairy chicken legs (because I could not see to shave, and even if I could, I could no longer balance on one leg), I said a little prayer that you would come early. That maybe we calculated wrong, and you really weren't a Wildstock baby. (What can I say? The national Wild Oats conference was in Vegas that year, and things got a little crazy.) Yes, I was sure, the labor pains would start any minute.

But the days dragged on, and the labor pains did not come. Now, don't get me wrong, honey—I loved you then and I love you now, but by the time Christmas arrived, I was over it. The pregnancy thing, I mean. I wanted to see my toes again, to bend over without falling down, sit and not have to think about who was there to help me back up. And you still didn't come. Looking back, I think maybe you were just trying to establish a system of hierarchy in which you reigned queen. Yes, that must have been it, because still you never miss an opportunity to remind me who is really in charge. All day long, legs wrapped firmly around my waist as I heft you around, I follow your pointing finger while you direct me, speaking in tongues.

For months I had been heaving this belly around, and I was tired of folks stopping me in the street pointing with big fingers and loud voices: "Whoooah! You're about ready to pop, there, aren't you?" And the look of surprise on their faces when I answered, "No, still got three more months to go." "That one's comin' early," the wise-looking women would always say, shaking their heads. Little kids would run away from me and grab their mamas' legs, afraid, I suppose, of my belly the way Indiana Jones was afraid of the speeding boulder in the cave. "Ooooh, honey," they'd all say, "that's a boy in there. No doubt about it."

So you set out to prove the world wrong before you even dried your body of amniotic fluid.

I went to sleep each night hoping midnight would wake me with shots of life through my belly. December 28 came, the day the little wheel in the midwife's kit said you were supposed to come, and then it went, leaving nothing but twenty-four more aggravated hours of anticipation. Then the twenty-ninth, the thirtieth, and the thirty-first, and we knew then that our little lovebug would lead us into a new year instead of wrapping one up. I can safely say, my dear, that you are a leader.

As I waited, I heard stories of women who went a week, two weeks, three, and four past their due dates. I tried not to cry each time a "sympathetic" mother exclaimed in the grocery store, "Oh honey, my son was nineteen days late!" I nearly jumped for joy when our midwife, Alice, told me that, technically, I was in labor when I called to let her know that I had lost part of my mucous plug. I ate a good meal and drank lots of water and tried to pretend not to think about it. I had casual discussions with supermarket cashiers, smiling to myself because they didn't know my secret: the contractions were sure to start within the hour, or surely by evening. But they didn't. After a few days off during the holidays, your daddy went back to work and called us every morning to check our status. And every day I told him the same thing, sitting in my glider recliner, watching ER reruns. Nothing. Nada. Stubborn little shrimp.

Your bubi was nearly as anxious as me, and called as often as daddy. I was sure I would be swollen and fat forever, that I would spend the rest of my life sleeping on my side and hearing floorboards groan under my weight whenever I walked on them. Every day I would answer the multitude of calls from excited family and friends with a somber, "No, not yet." I could see this never ending. I tried acupuncture, black cohosh, walking, and sex, but nothing worked. The oven was on and you weren't done cooking. Your bubi and I spent those last few days getting manicures and pedicures, her trying to make me feel beautiful despite my acned shoulders and swollen ankles (ironic how the utmost symbol of fertility and femininity can also be the utter opposite: your hairy, sweaty, swollen self making even the temptation to shirk your motherly duties and run off into the sunset with Mr. Right an impossibility). Her sincere efforts were appreciated, and they even managed to help me forget about my longing to pop, although by then I was sure you would continue to grow inside me until the greater part of your teenage years were over, anyway. Which actually might not have been so bad, come to think of it.

You were due to arrive on a Saturday. Six days later I was still waiting. It was a Friday morning, your father had gone off to work, and I was madly baking cookies and trying not to think about how much I wanted this belly full of baby to turn into an armful of baby. I spent the morning mixing ingredients for a treat I planned on freezing, since my middle had grown so large we were a little worried about how big you might be getting. All it took was one thought about trying to push a ten-pound baby out at home to make all the sweetness of chocolate chip cookies fade away. Around 11 a.m., your daddy called to see how everything was going. I'm not sure what it was, but something in the waiting and the wanting broke me, and as I burst into tears, I told him that I just couldn't do it anymore. I wept my exhaustion on the phone, felt desperate with wanting and a mile past ready. He heard my cries and decided to leave work, come home, and be with us. And as I hung up the phone I had a thought: in birthing class, I learned that when a woman finally says, "I can't do this anymore" during her labor, she usually doesn't have to. It is at that very point, when her body has stretched itself to the absolute maximum limits, beyond anything she ever thought possible, that it reels itself back in and the baby begins to emerge. And upon remembering this, I thought that maybe this was it. Maybe just when I became so desperate I honestly felt I could no longer carry this load, the load would magically be lifted.

Your father came home and we went to the movies. We saw A Beautiful Mind. The whole time you kicked and danced inside me. We came home, and soon after I fell asleep. Your father sat on the living room couch and enjoyed his final solitary evening of watching TV for a long while to come.

I heard him collapse into bed at around one thirty in the morning. I heard him because a pain in my stomach had woken me up. By now I had had so many false starts that I knew not to wake him until I was sure. And so I told myself it was those darn Braxton-Hicks contractions again, and to try to sleep through them. But after about half an hour of feeling them every so often, too strong to close my eyes anymore and yet not strong enough to be convinced, I decided to open my eyes and time them by the alarm clock on the nightstand next to the bed. The nightstand was a hand-me-down from the home where your Grandpa John, for whom you are named, grew up in. They were coming every ten minutes or so. And while they were nothing I couldn't handle, they certainly had a new air of strength to them. At 2 a.m. I woke your papa up. He hadn't really been to sleep yet, and in his utter exhaustion he rolled over, eyes still closed, and told me to try to get some sleep. Clearly, he had never been in labor before. Neither had all those folks in our getting-ready-for-baby class who suggested this as a rational possibility in early labor. Realizing that it was he who was actually the delirious one with that comment, I collected myself and, with a deep breath, woke him once again in the sweetest "about-to-go-through-the-most-painful-experience-of-my-life" voice and told him it was time. And then he was up.

We counted through contractions, timed the spaces in between, and wondered if this was it. An hour later we decided that indeed it was, and prepared ourselves for what we expected to be a grueling day or two. Not too much later, I began bleeding; this prompted a call to our midwife, Alice, who confirmed that labor had begun, told us we were in for a long haul, and gave me permission to soak in the bathtub. I hobbled into our little bathroom and watched the water fill the tub, then as gingerly as a woman nine and a half months pregnant could possibly be, I stepped in and was lost to hot water. Your father sat on the edge of the tub with a stopwatch and waited for my signal each time a contraction began. We struggled through a meager attempt at breathing exercises, for it wasn't until I was comfortably (?) situated in the bathtub and well into active labor that we chose to learn the techniques. So I sat with a belly full of baby and he sat perched on the edge of a very small tub in a very small bathroom, and, when my uterus relaxed, read aloud from a book

about how to breathe. He would pant, quickly or slowly depending on what the book suggested, and I would open my mouth,
stick out my tongue, and copy him. It wasn't the most opportune
time to decide to be a student, though, and we quickly aban-
doned the idea and relied on instinct. Which seemed to work just
fine, by the way.

The contractions came harder and closer together, and I
wriggled and waggled between the porcelain walls of my container. It was a tight squeeze, but each attempt at waterless positions failed miserably and always I ended up back where I started. It was around this time that your father realized he probably
should have read the directions on how to erect the birthing tub
we had sitting in pieces on our bedroom floor. My memory
became a little fuzzy at this point, but imagine this: I am naked
and immersed in water (at least all of me that fits). The labor has
progressed considerably, and your father is running between the
living room and the bathroom frantically attempting to piece
together a small Jacuzzi-sized tub in a room not much bigger
than a Jacuzzi and listening for me to calmly yell, "Riiiiichhhh,"
thus signaling the beginning of the next contraction. With each
one, he comes running back to sit with me through it, then, anxious not to waste another second, runs out until he hears my call.

I was surprisingly calm through the entire ordeal. The night
was quickly becoming morning, and as the weekend dawned,
something significant changed. I couldn't put my finger on
exactly what it was, but it was more than just a harder, longer
moan from within my body. Your song had hit a high note, and
the music we were making suddenly was making us.

I had done all the things laboring women do; I huffed and I
puffed, and as I lay nearly naked in a tub full of warm water, I
felt you move in me. You moved through my body like a tidal
wave, and though there must have been a part so sad to see you
leave, the pieces obliged and let you through. I felt my own con-
struction change, and it wasn't until the earthquake moved me
that I even recognized where each piece was to begin with. A little over eight hours after I first woke up your daddy, I was lying
on my back against him in a pool of warm water magically con-
structed in our very little living room when you slithered out

from between my legs and into your bubi's waiting arms. And in a room where I am sure there were a thousand voices laughing and crying at the wonder that was you, I can only remember your wet body on my breast as my nose pressed into your little bald head and smelled you for the very first time. In that moment, there was only me and you.

In the hustle and bustle of the next few hours I can only tell you that your uncles arrived to hold together the water that I so needed, your daddy held me, your bubi held me in her stare, and Alice held down the house. And at 11:03 in the morning, I held you, wrapped in the flannel of your Grandpa John's favorite shirt. That was a night that woke up to a whole new world. We did good work, you and I. I moaned and I groaned and I sang out a baby; you danced a harmony, and together we led the choir around us into the most beautiful crescendo.

I am so happy you are here.

Abigail Dotson writes: *I live in the Santa Cruz Mountains with my nineteen-month-old daughter, Ruby Jane, and her papa. Most days we spend frolicking under a canopy of redwoods and hunting banana slugs. Sometimes we find a poem hidden in the trees or on the road; sometimes we find a story; sometimes we just find fun. (Abigail's writing has appeared on www.mothering.com.)*

MY VBAC ODYSSEY

Amy Galarowicz

No matter how "stuck in a rut" I feel at times, I marvel that I have changed so much in only two or four years. Motherhood has been such an amazing journey for me. I can't help giggling at things I do differently with my one-year-old son versus his four-year-old brother. Among other things, this piece is about their very different birth stories.

First a little background. My first son was born amid fear, timidity, IVs, epidurals, and glaring lights; and alas, in a surgical suite. Even as it happened, I felt as if I were huddling in the corner as an onlooker; I was so detached from the whole process. I immediately vowed to not be so ignorant and helpless the next time around.

Somehow, my first son nursed well through the haze of postpartum, and onward past his second birthday. Unwittingly, I started to buck other "society norms," just learning to follow my heart wherever my beautiful son was concerned. He didn't sleep through the night for quite a while; forcing him to "cry it out" just seemed wrong, despite the advice of many who suggested we try it. I enjoyed cooking, so why on earth wouldn't I cook his first solid foods? After getting a vaccine that was later pulled off the market, I read up on that issue.

When he was a year old, I discovered *Mothering* magazine, and I joined a community of other moms like me. How validating! I was encouraged by an article about the importance of modern mommas finding (or creating) "their tribe." I set about doing that, when I wasn't learning things from my son.

Fast forward through two more years of learning and growing. When, last spring, I made it through my first trimester, I

119

vowed things would be different for this pregnancy. In a most timely way, Mothering magazine dedicated an issue to VBAC births, and it kicked off my research phase. After learning more, I realized I wanted to respect my baby and my body in ways I knew my OB-GYNs were not prepared to support; they had to go. Personally, I was thinking midwife and/or water- and home birth, but my husband disagreed. Our compromise was to birth the baby in a hospital, but with the help of a doula and hip doctor. So, I figured, I'll ask around and find an area OB-GYN who was less scalpel-happy. No problem.

Well, I asked everyone I knew. I networked with relaxed moms I know, midwives, doulas, breastfeeders, and more. It really started to concern me that so few names were coming up at all. Surely amongst four million people in North Jersey, there had to be one doctor who was willing to trust a woman's body to do its own thing. I realized that finding local resources to support moms like me was not easy. Over the course of my desperate search, I connected with some really neat ladies, and it got me thinking. Why should I settle for a "virtual" community of like-minded moms who gather together, share, and support one another through a magazine? Why not start a support group where we get together in person? By the time I was in my last trimester, the Holistic Moms Network was born.

Having been blessed with all the resources we needed (and a few angels in my life) it came together quite quickly. Two brave moms came forward immediately as co-leaders, seeing that I needed to work myself out of the job quickly once baby was born. Then, my chiropractor let us use his office for meetings, and a buddy first volunteered to set up an e-mail loop, then later taught me how to run it myself. So, for over a year now, we've been getting together one evening a month in person. We educate, inspire, and support one another. We often have speakers, but keep their talks brief so that we can network afterward. Naturally, nurslings of any age are welcome at our meetings. Some of our focus topics have included vaccinations, nutritional herbs, organic lawn care, holistic dentistry, good fats versus bad fats, feng shui, and more. We also meet during the day for playgroups, as well as through our e-mail discussion loop. Just as we hoped, it has been tremendously validating to simply be in a room with other moms like us.

Since May 2002, we have consistently grown. We presently meet in Cedar Grove, New Jersey, but hope to be spinning off a Bergen County, New Jersey group by the end of this year. We post a few flyers around, but for the most part, we run without money. Through the free e-mail loop, we send meeting reminders, post meeting notes, share news of upcoming area events, discuss current headlines, etc. For many of us, we have finally found our "tribe." How cool is that?

But back to my birth journey. It was amazing this time around, never mind mostly conscious! I finally did find a wonderful OB-GYN. I didn't mind the thirty-plus minute drive to get to Dr. Judy's office, because there was a Trader Joe's nearby and I could shop there every time I had a checkup. And my doula! Mere words cannot express how grateful I am to Memory for so totally "being there" in ways too numerous to recount. Start to finish, all twenty-two hours, she was there with me, helping me reach my goal of labor and birth with less intervention. And most of all, I appreciated my husband, the love of my life, for supporting me even though he did not understand some of my choices. (I still think having a birth doula is totally a chick thing, and some men will never "get it.") In the end, I delivered my precious baby with minimal difficulties. Not the doctors. Not the equipment or drugs. I did it! Wow. I will never forget it.

Amy Galarowicz writes: *I have two beautiful boys—Walter, aged one year, and big brother Lou at four and a half (just ask him, he'll tell you). I've always been a community-oriented, networking kind of girl; however, since becoming a mom, I've sought "my tribe" with a vengeance. I've moved from professional societies to church groups and now to moms' groups—what a ride! With mixed feelings, I'm fixin' to launch back into the part-time work world in autumn, 2003. As always, I look forward to whatever God brings me next.*

WITH A LITTLE HELP FROM YOUR FRIENDS

Tina K. Mott

Friends, especially the ones who support the kind of birth you want, are essential. I, for one, am blessed to have a group of girlfriends who provided me with endless encouragement and love. I know that Sofia's birth would have not been such a beautiful experience had it not been for this group of friends. After announcing the pregnancy, they bought books and a breastfeeding doll for Tessa, my (then) two-year-old. We read the books all the time and it really helped Tessa with the big transition.

With their encouragement, I went weekly to see a chiropractor, Dr. Donna, who later convinced me that I had been able to push out a ten-pound baby in thirty minutes because my pelvis had such good shape. One friend got me interested in making and drinking an herbal pregnancy tea. I also became connected with many wonderful women in the birthing community: my midwife, doulas, etc. And towards the end of my pregnancy, my girlfriends held a blessing way ceremony for me, at which each woman, instead of gifts, gave me a blessing or wish they had for me during my pregnancy and birth. It was magical, and I will never forget it. They handed out candles to everyone, and when my labor began, I called my friend, Kathy, who began a phone chain to the rest of the group. It was an incredible source of strength and comfort to know they all had candles burning in their homes during my birthing journey.

Here is the brief version of the labor and delivery. On Monday night, I began having serious cramps. I had been crampy for about a week, and analyzed every little sensation in my body, because I was now over a week overdue, which felt like months overdue. That morning I had been to my midwife for a checkup and decided (after much contemplation) to get checked—she said that I was three centimeters and eighty percent effaced, and she thought that this baby was coming either that day, Monday, or Tuesday. I was so excited.

So, around midnight on Monday, I started timing the cramps and noticed that they came every five to nine minutes, but were pretty regular. I stayed in bed and could not sleep because the contractions were too painful. I never woke up my husband Doug, thinking I would let him sleep until I really needed him (thanks to advice from my Bradley instructor). They stayed the same strength and varied from five to nine minutes apart. The following morning around 6 a.m., the contractions totally stopped. I was so bummed and exhausted. Since I was tired, I asked my mom to watch Tessa while I tried to snooze. So, I got some sleep on Tuesday morning, but no labor. Doug was home that day, and when I woke up in late morning, I felt like walking. It was freezing outside, so I dragged him to the mall (Doug hates malls!) and we walked. The contractions started again sometime around 1 p.m.

That afternoon, I had an appointment to get an ultrasound at Morristown Memorial Hospital because I was so overdue, just to check the fluid, placenta, etc. I called my midwife and asked her if I should go, even though I was having contractions. Since they weren't that strong, she wanted us to go just to make sure everything was okay. So, at 3 p.m., we went to the hospital. By this point, the contractions were thirty seconds long and about five minutes apart. I had to focus on each contraction (they were getting more intense), but I was still feeling pretty good. At Morristown, they freaked out that I was in labor, and wanted to send me directly to Labor and Delivery. After much back and forth, with our midwife on the cell phone, we marched out of there, Against Medical Advice! We never got the ultrasound. We decided to go home, make a fire, eat something, and just see what happened. On the way, we stopped by our homeopath's office to pick up a homeopathic labor kit. I immediately took one of the remedies, and I believe it really helped get things moving.

I missed Tessa a lot during labor. She had been at my parents' house since that morning and, being overemotional, I wanted to see her before the baby was born. So, my parents came over around 6 p.m. with Tessa. She knew what was going on, and was worried about her mommy during the contractions. (She still "plays labor" and bends over, grunting!) I was so happy to see her and hug her.

At 6 p.m., we also asked my doula to come over. I was having very regular contractions—every four to five minutes, around thirty to forty seconds long. My contractions never got to be longer than that, which I think saved me, because by the time the contraction was too painful to bear, it started to go away. So, my doula arrived that evening, and we just labored at home. The biggest challenge was finding comfortable positions to deal with the contractions.

My contractions slammed me, and I never really knew when they would hit, so Doug let me know by looking at his watch, estimating, and then giving me a warning. A small word about Doug—he is an artist by profession and in his heart and spirit. (Hint: practical/organizational stuff is not his strength.) I was concerned that he would not be able to handle all the responsibility of labor, like remembering to time the contractions and all the comfort measures we had learned. But he was amazing! In fact, more than my doula, I wanted his arms around me, his breath in my ear, and his words of support during the contractions. I wanted him and only him to help me. And he was totally there for me. There is no way I could have gotten through this without him.

Around 11 p.m. we left for the hospital. I have no idea how this decision was made. In my mind, I had no idea how far along I was and was just getting restless. I thought it might be "fun" to try out the tub at the hospital, and I was impatient about being at home. So, it took a while to get packed up, and Doug set up a nice comfy backseat for me. I was surprised how comfortable I was in the car, just saying to myself that I only had to get through six or so contractions until we got to the hospital. We got there around midnight, and after I checked in and changed, my midwife (who, by the way, was not on call that evening, but made a special effort to deliver Sofia, anyway) checked me and said that I was just about nine centimeters! Doug and my doula were

floored, but I was in such a trance by that point that I just wanted it all to be over. It was too late for the tub.

Then, at about twelve thirty, my water broke, and the contractions came like tidal waves. Up until this point, I really felt
that I could handle it all—one contraction at a time—just breathing through them, patiently trying to relax. After my water
broke, the pain was overwhelming and no position was comfortable. I tried sitting on the toilet, squatting, everything. My midwife and doula encouraged me to push, but I could not bear the
thought of pushing-pain on top of the contraction-pain.

But then, my midwife announced that she could see the
baby's head—without any pushing!—and during the contractions, the heart rate was going down to one hundred. When I
heard that, and saw the joy on Doug's face, I pushed with all my
might. They asked me if I wanted the mirror—I said no way!
They asked me if I wanted to touch the head—still, no way! I
couldn't focus on anything besides pushing the baby out. I never
got the "urge" to push. I just wanted it to be over.

At 1:23 a.m., December 11 (by the way, my birthday is May
11, and Tessa's is September 11), Sofia Barbara Mott was born,
weighing nine pounds and ten ounces, and measuring twenty-
one inches.

Doug announced that we had another girl. My midwife had
to suction her immediately, due to some meconium. The cord
was very short, so she rested Sofia on my lower belly until the
cord stopped pulsing. Then Doug cut the cord, ripped off his
shirt, and snuggled his newest little angel skin to skin. (I think
the nurse was wondering why this man was undressing!) Then,
I had to be stitched up from some minor tearing—about six very
painful stitches.

I finally got to hold Sofia, put her on my breast, and examine our beautiful baby. She was so peaceful and big. I was
exhausted, but elated. I had the shakes very badly, and it took me
several hours to realize what had just happened. Doug said that I
acted very similarly to how I was after the cesarean with Tessa,
coming off the medication, except this time it was my body's
own medication. Looking back, the "self medication" was probably the only way I could deal with the whole experience. All the

things I thought I would worry about—the baby's health, it being a VBAC, for example—I never did. I was so absorbed in the experience of giving birth. The profoundness of it all is still only beginning to hit me.

After the birth, Doug and I sat there with Sofia until 5 a.m., chatting with our midwife and doula before they went home, and just relishing the miracle we had experienced. Then we called our families to share the good news. I thought I would be on the phone immediately with my parents, but for some reason, it just felt right to be present and alone with my new daughter and husband.

I will never be able to fully thank my girlfriends for everything they provided to welcome Sofia into this world. Hopefully they know that they were all part of this sacred journey.

Tina Mott *is the mother of two girls, Tessa and Sofia, and wife of Douglas, photographer (www.douglasmott.com), all living in Chatham, New Jersey.*

BREASTFEEDING IS BEST FEEDING

BREASTFEEDING

Abigail Dotson

When I found out I was going to become a mom, there were a lot of things to consider. I had to think about whether or not I wanted to immunize, who would be at my birth, and what to name the baby. I thought about whether I would quit working altogether or try to work from home, whom to invite to the birth, and whether or not to give my newborn vitamin K. But there were some things that were a given from the moment I stood in my OB-GYN's office and heard her tell me I was pregnant: I would have a home birth, I would sleep with my baby, and I would breastfeed. Forever, if I could.

So from the moment that sweet little pea slid out of my body and latched on, I was as hooked as she. I couldn't really imagine that there would be folks who would be offended by my tendency to whip 'em out at any given moment, sort of like how when I was growing up I couldn't imagine that there were really Republicans and that I would ever meet one. And so I approached public breastfeeding with an almost "I dare you" sort of philosophy. I was a firm believer in feeding on demand from the very beginning, and if my daughter wanted to nurse right at the moment I happened to be standing in the checkout line at the supermarket, then the formula-feeding mother of four behind me and the Harley Davidson rider in front of me were just going to have to be privy to our not-so-private moment. I could often be seen wheeling her stroller with one hand as I walked down the beach, cradling my suckling daughter at my bosom. It doesn't take long to learn how to use your two hands as if they are four when you're a breastfeeding mother.

There were certainly stares, and the occasional nudge to a friend as strangers passed me and my breasts in public venues. I let the obscene comment of a teenager or two roll off my shoulders (only because they were teenagers), feeling sad that seeing a breastfeeding woman as nature intended her was cause enough to incite such nasty comments in the new millennium's generation of kids. I wondered what that said about our society. If nothing else, it said that not enough women are either breastfeeding at all, or comfortable enough doing it publicly to normalize the experience for those around us. And sadly, this directly affects our children. When we are uncomfortable breastfeeding, we will turn more quickly to alternate forms of nourishment, forsaking the ultimate nutritional and bonding value of breast milk for bottles (even those who choose to pump are robbing themselves and their children of the many other benefits of breastfeeding).

As those of you who've breastfed children yourselves already know, it takes a little time to really get the knack of it. So in the beginning, I must admit, my grace was suffering and often I stumbled through the experience, unable to successfully lift one side of my shirt without lifting the other, accidentally untying the bow on my postpartum drawstring pants, not to mention needing to expose the entire breast just to get my daughter to the nipple. But these things happen, and with a little practice, we soon became an expert team. I could push the stroller, browse the new releases at our local bookstore, carry on a cell phone conversation, and nurse the baby all at the same time. Most mothers can.

With time, nursing became second nature to me, and I suppose like every nursing mother these days I was confronted with a certain facet of society who was "not-so-supportive" of public breastfeeding. Like a true Sagittarian, I was ready to rumble. I confess there was a part of me that almost couldn't wait for the man in the bank to call me a "f—ing rodent" as I sat on a sofa quietly nursing my baby girl. I knew what to say to him; I had it all rehearsed in my head. I almost *wanted* to get kicked out of a restaurant, just so I could give the manager a piece of my mind. I would defend my right to breastfeed with a patriotic gusto, vehement in my pro-breastfeeding stand. When confronted with such blatant disapproval, I knew exactly what to say and stood on strong ground.

The problem came from a less likely place. I had anticipated the angry passersby and disgusted store owners; what I had not prepared for was the onslaught of subtle disapproval cleverly disguised as support. I did not question my motives, my exposed breast, or my timing when openly harassed. It wasn't until a kindly woman asked me if I would like her to show me to a more private corner that I began to feel ill at ease. Until then, it hadn't occurred to me that many rational people—people who believed wholeheartedly in breastfeeding—expected that I would prefer privacy. Her well-wishing concern gave me my first dose of self-consciousness around the issue, as if someone had suddenly pointed out that there was something to feel awkward about where before there had been nothing. While it is words like hers that have led me to examine this very issue, I am hopeful that one day our society as a whole can return to the place of my previous naïveté.

When I was approached by an angry man one day who shouted obscenities at me and my nursing daughter, onlookers were quick to intercede on my behalf. I was not afraid, nor was I tempted to give his accusations a second thought. When, however, an employee later asked me how come I didn't tell her I was going to do "that" so she could have let me use a back office, I quickly wondered if I should have. It was the well-wisher who made me question my actions, and it is exactly this kind of statement that reflects a society largely uncomfortable with the idea that breasts are multifunctional. Most importantly they are an instrument of sustenance and a means of nourishing our young, although in the wake of their own revolution we seem to have forsaken this foremost purpose for one purely sexual. We witness breasts bared in nearly imagined bikini tops; we walk around malls and are confronted with posters advertising women's lingerie, bathing suits, and blouses cut to accentuate the cleavage. And hidden among these blatantly sexual depictions is the lone maternity store, proudly displaying an enlarged photograph of a sensibly dressed woman in a nursing shirt cleverly designed to hide her breasts. As though now that they are suddenly useful for something more than a wet T-shirt contest we should forget we have them. Now don't get me wrong; I am a big fan of the breast. But I am a fan of the breast in all its glory. There are many faces to each woman's own, and I am as proud of the ones I have now as I was of those I had ten years ago. Please, don't make me feel ashamed to put them to their rightful use. As a mother I am expected to care for my child as best as I can, and yet I am bombarded with criticism for doing exactly that.

It is seldom the ignorant and angry public who intimidate this breastfeeding mom, but the kindly folk who think they are doing a good thing by propagating the idea that breastfeeding should be a private experience. Our breasts, in the end, have been so sexualized that even those with the best intent cannot separate their sexuality from their functionality. Even those of us who choose to integrate ourselves into communities that embrace our choice to breastfeed are hammered with advertisements for clothing offering "discreet" access. The world around us is telling us over and over again that they don't want to see our breasts (at least not until we are finished breastfeeding and then only if they are still adequately perky), that we should hide them, that breastfeeding is a public issue when in reality it has as much to do with those who happen to be around you as what you ate for breakfast. The only people who should be concerned about how you breastfeed are your child and yourself, and whether the concern of others manifests itself in an angry or a "helpful" way, as breastfeeding women, we should learn to ignore it all.

I'm tired of slings that allow you to breastfeed with minimum breast exposure; I'm tired of being offered a blanket or a jacket to "cover up" with; I'm tired of being asked to pay an arm and a leg for clothing with slits on the chest permitting one to breastfeed while their breasts remain covered. I'm proud of my breasts and their ability to nourish my daughter; I love the way she fondles and molds them as she nurses, the way she stops every so often to say, "Hi, mama," and smile or coo (thereby, god forbid, letting my entire breast hang free for all who pass to see!). I don't expect her to eat under a blanket or slurp continuously until she is done, never pausing for conversation. My daughter eats the same way I do (or at least did, before I had a baby to care for!): slowly, socially, and savoring each bite. What she has for lunch is as much your business as what you have for lunch is hers. Let us nurse in peace, however and wherever we choose to do it.

Abigail Dotson writes: *I live in the Santa Cruz mountains with my nineteen-month-old daughter, Ruby Jane, and her papa. Most days we spend frolicking under a canopy of redwoods and hunting banana slugs. Sometimes we find a poem hidden in the trees or on the road; sometimes we find a story; sometimes we just find fun. (Abigail's writing has appeared on www.mothering.com.)*

SUPPORTING OUR BABIES, SHOWING OUR BREASTS

Sarah J. Buckley

The Federation of Commercial TV Stations has performed a welcome back-flip on its rating of an Australian Breastfeeding Association (ABA) Community Service Announcement, which shows a mother breastfeeding her baby (CM 20/3). Its initial assessment and PG rating, with the implication that the sight of "too much breast" might disturb a young child, has now been modified to a G rating, but this process has exposed some deepseated attitudes towards women's breasts and the act of breastfeeding, that, to my mind, verge on "mammophobia."

Perhaps the ruling agency was unaware that we are a mammalian species—that is, we are defined by our mammaries (breasts) and their ability to nourish and nurture our young. Further, with the average age of weaning worldwide estimated at 4.2 years, the agency initially assumed that children who are young enough to breastfeed are not old enough to see a woman's breast performing its natural, mammalian function on TV.

As a GP, writer, and mother of four children, all long-term breastfeeders, I feel sad that these attitudes are still so strong in our culture. Scantily clad women's bodies in sexually provocative poses can be on public display, but we remain uncomfortable about showing our breasts in public to feed our babies. This attitude is very specific to Western cultures—even in Muslim countries, fully veiled women have no embarrassment about exposing a breast to feed a hungry baby in a public place. It is exactly this misplaced discomfort that the ABA is wanting to counter with this thirty-second ad, due to be released this week.

This is, I believe, a major public health issue. As Baumslag and Michels note in their book, *Milk, Money and Madness* (Bergin and Garvey 1995), "When women start feeling self-conscious about exposure of their breasts, they start thinking about other ways to feed their infants." And so the formula companies find a niche to appropriate, moving in with their huge budgets and forceful marketing practices. In Australia, around twelve percent of babies are formula-fed from birth, but by six months, more than fifty percent of babies are being raised in nonhuman milk.

This lack of breastfeeding is producing a huge burden of disease in our community. Babies who are not breastfed have higher rates of hospitalization and death in their first year, even in developed countries. They also are more likely to suffer from SIDS, diarrheal and respiratory illnesses, bacterial meningitis, ear infections, allergies, asthma, urinary infections, inguinal hernias, childhood lymphomas (cancers), juvenile diabetes, coeliac disease, juvenile rheumatoid arthritis, reflux, dental cavities, and malocclusion, and to have poorer speech development, slower social development, lower IQ, and lower school grades than their breastfed peers.

As they grow into adulthood, non-breastfed individuals are also at increased risk of inflammatory bowel disease (Crohn's disease and ulcerative colitis), multiple sclerosis, and cardiovascular disease. Adults who have never been breastfed are six times more likely to be obese than those who were breastfed for more than twelve months, and non-breastfed females are thirty-three percent more likely to develop breast cancer. Cancers of the ovary and endometrium (uterus) are also more common in non-breastfed females.

Breastfeeding offers major health benefits to us as mothers. For example, we reduce our own risk of breast cancer by twenty-five percent for every six months that we breastfeed, and we have a lower chance of osteoporosis—thinning bones—in older age. Breastfeeding also gives us the benefits that come with a delay in the return of our fertile cycles, such as less chance of conception and better iron levels because of delayed menstruation.

As well as all of the above health benefits, breastfeeding offers other intrinsic rewards to mothers and babies. For all mammals, these include the effects of the breastfeeding hormones oxytocin, the hormone of love; endorphins, hormones of pleasure; and prolactin, the mothering hormone. These hormones, which we release each time we breastfeed, keep us calm, relaxed, and lovingly focused on our babies, and our babies also receive love and pleasure via the oxytocin and endorphins in our breast milk.

The act of breastfeeding also gives our babies holding, touch, skin-to-skin contact; visual, oral, and tactile stimulation; and deep-seated security—some writers have described breast milk as liquid love. Erasmus Darwin—Charles's grandfather—credits a baby's suckling pleasure (and mechanism) for the origin of our human smile.

In short, breastfeeding is the one of the most effective preventative health measures that exists, and it offers the best that nature can give for mothers and for babies.

If breastfeeding were a commercial intervention, backed by big business, its benefits would be loudly proclaimed, and our breasts would be extolled for their beautiful and miraculous functions. Television would be replete with images of mothers breastfeeding their babies at all times of the day, and we would all smile—adults and children alike—when we saw a woman breastfeeding her baby in public.

Breastfeeding is supported in our culture, but not as well as it could be. Community attitudes need to shift, and the ad produced for the ABA is a wonderful start. I look forward to the time when we appreciate, as do our Muslim sisters, that breastfeeding is the right of every baby, and that the benefits and pleasures of the breastfeeding relationship provide, naturally, our nourishment for a lifetime.

Sarah J. Buckley is a trained GP (family MD), writer, and mother to Emma (thirteen), Zoe (ten), Jacob (eight) and Maia (three), all born ecstatically at home. Her writing on pregnancy, birth, and parenting has been published internationally, and she is currently writing a book about ecstatic birth. She lives in Brisbane, Australia with Nicholas, the love of her life. You can read more of her articles at www.womenofspirit.asn.au/sarahjbuckley.html, and you can e-mail her at sarahjbuckley@uqconnect.net

THE BENEFITS OF EXTENDED NURSING THAT NO STUDY CAN QUANTIFY

Kim Collins

When I had my first son five and three-quarters (he would want to be sure to say the three-quarters!) years ago, I had no idea that I would nurse him for nearly three years. I hoped for three months—that seemed reasonable. This was the year before the advisory to nurse at least a year or two, and by the time the information came out, we had surpassed the year mark. But back to the start. It was natural, so it should come naturally, right? Well, it didn't—not really, not for us at first. Fortunately, my doula had whispered to me as I put my boy, Leo, to my breast moments after he was born, "Okay, get ready for nursing boot camp—it might be tough for a bit, but it will come together," and she was right.

This is horrible to admit, but I spent a few days praying for some infection that would make it impossible to continue feeding. My husband was terrific, and he went out and bought nursing books, cabbage, teas, and creams. What he did not buy was formula. He called our doula for help. They sat up with me and helped me until we got it right.

We were a nursing couple until just before his third birthday, when he informed me that "Na Nas" were "broken." My milk was changing or diminishing because I was pregnant again. Anyway, that slowed things way down. He nursed only sometimes after that, including when the new milk for his baby brother was there. By then, he only took a slurp or two before giggling and stopping.

Now I am nursing my two-and-a-half-year-old boy, Oliver. And something amazing is happening: we talk about it! He is more verbal than Leo was at his age. And he is developing manners—nursing etiquette. He asks, "Na Nas, please" (yes, somehow he calls them the same thing). Sometimes he just wants to touch and is happy to have my husband's nipples as well! When he nurses, he now says, "Yummy! Thank you, Momma." I recently asked him what the milk tasted like, and he basically asked me why I didn't just taste it myself! But then he said they tasted like a lollipop, and then reconsidered and said, "No, Psycho Pop!" a favorite lollipop that he had only once, some time ago—a very sophisticated lollipop that is lots of flavors all together.

We all are aware of the health benefits and the basic bonding benefits of breastfeeding. But I never anticipated the benefit of being thanked in words and getting a little glimpse from him, in his own words, about how he experiences our nursing relationship. I feel so blessed to be having such conversations with my boy.

Kim Collins is a mother to two sons, Leo and Oliver, and wife to Len. Formerly an attorney, she now operates DoulaMomma Childbirth Services, serving as labor doula, childbirth educator, mentor, and bellycaster to mommas and their families. When a rare free moment appears, Kim loves to ski, travel, read, and hang out with the many wise women and kids whom she has the privilege of knowing.

NOT BORN OF MY BODY, BUT NURTURED AT MY BREASTS

Janet Tilden

My husband, Tom, and I have two sons. The older one, Jonathan, emerged from my body on September 24, 1987. Our younger son, Philip, was born on November 21, 1998 to a loving mother who was already raising three little boys by herself. She decided to place her fourth child for adoption, and we were blessed to become his parents when he was twenty-two days old.

Our path to adoption had been long and difficult. After Jonathan was weaned at three years and nine months, we began "trying" to have a second baby. I became pregnant in 1992 and miscarried near the end of the first trimester. The loss was difficult for all three of us, including four-year-old Jon, who had proclaimed proudly to everyone he met, including the clerk at the supermarket, "I'm going to be a big brother!" Two years later, I became pregnant again and miscarried once more. My husband and I underwent some preliminary testing for infertility in 1996, and we were disheartened by the expense and regimentation of infertility treatment, as well as the uncertainty of the outcome. We began to consider adoption as an alternative route to expanding our family.

At first, I felt that it would be best to adopt a child of three or four. Having had a wonderful nursing experience with my first son, I could not imagine bottle-feeding a baby. Nursing was such an integral part of my mothering that I could not picture myself comforting a fussy baby with a plastic nipple. We considered adopting from Russia, and we were discouraged by the costs and paperwork involved. Next, we looked into Guatemalan adoption. We paid the application fee to a Guatemalan orphanage, then were notified that the rates would be double what we'd originally been told. Back to square one, but still eager to adopt, we found an agency in our area that would help us find a child.

Our agency, Adoption Links Worldwide, held one-and-a-half-day workshops for prospective parents. On the second day of our workshop during the spring of 1998, several adoptive families brought their children and spoke to the group about their experiences. The children included a little boy from Romania, a little girl from China, another boy from Vietnam, and a little boy who had been born in Florida to black parents and adopted by a single white woman. All of the children were beautiful, but my eyes kept returning to the little toddler who was black—he was adorable, bright, and full of personality. I wanted to pick him up and hug him. On the way home from the workshop, my husband and I began to talk about adopting a child who was black. It was an intriguing idea, and we decided to look into the possibility.

A little while later, during one of our home study interviews, my husband told the social worker that he preferred to adopt a baby rather than a toddler or preschool-aged child. He felt that attachment would be much easier with a child who was adopted at birth. Lisa, our social worker, asked if we were open to the possibility of adopting a child who was black or biracial. We had been under the impression that trans-racial adoptive placements were rare and difficult, but our social worker told us that many black birth mothers were open to the possibility of placing their children with white adoptive parents. They wanted their children to have permanent, loving homes instead of growing up in foster care. We were told that many black families were adopting children, but there were not enough black families for all the children who needed homes. We told Lisa that we were open to adopting a baby of any race. By this time, I had done some research on the Internet and discovered that it was possible to nurse an adopted baby. We wrote our "Dear Birthparent" letter and waited to hear from the adoption agency about a possible placement.

The summer months passed, and we began to get discouraged. How long would it take to get a referral? In September

1998, we decided to wait another year, then pursue international adoption. At the time, we were both forty years old and our older son had just turned eleven.

Two months later, right before Thanksgiving, I received a phone call from Lisa. She told me that a healthy baby boy had been born three days earlier in Mississippi to black parents, and the birth mother had signed the papers to place him for adoption. Were we interested in being considered by the birth mother? "Yes!" I told her eagerly. Two days later, we received another call, this time from Debbie, the director of the adoption agency in Mississippi. Debbie left a message on our answering machine, and I retrieved the message while we were visiting relatives in Illinois. Debbie's friendly voice announced that papers were being processed for our adoption, and she needed to know the adoptive mother's maiden name, the county in which we lived, and the name we had chosen for the baby. Suddenly, everything seemed very real to us. We were truly going to have another baby, and it would happen very soon!

The next three weeks seemed to drag on forever. Because we were adopting from another state, Interstate Compact paperwork had to be completed in both states before we could bring our baby home. Our baby would be in "cradle care" until the paperwork was finished. The birthfather had to sign relinquishment papers in front of a notary public, and government workers in both states had to process the adoption papers. In the meantime, I cried when I thought of the birth mother's loss, which reminded me of my own miscarriages. What was it like for her to leave the hospital with empty arms? What was it like for "my" baby to be separated from his birthmother? She had chosen not to hold him after he was born, and I suspected she made this decision because she was afraid that if she held him even for a few moments, she would never be able to let him go. She felt that adoption would give him the best chance for a happy future, and she did not want to jeopardize her decision.

During a long-distance telephone call, I spoke with the "cradle care" mother, Gwen, who told me that Philip was an adorable, "good" baby who loved to be held and would snuggle his little head under her chin when she picked him up. She said he had been spitting up a lot in the hospital, and he was put on a soy formula but was still spitting up quite a bit. I wanted to rush down to Mississippi, grab my baby, and bring him home immediately, but I had to wait. Meanwhile, I purchased baby supplies and rented a breast pump to get my nipples in shape for nursing. I worried that Philip might prefer bottles to my breasts. After doing an Internet search, I found a couple of websites devoted to adoptive nursing, and I learned a great deal from other mothers who had been there. I ordered a Lact-Aid nursing supplementer because it was recommended by many of the adoptive mothers who had been successful in nursing their babies.

Finally we learned that the paperwork was nearly complete, and we would be able to bring our baby home within a few days. Jonathan was worried about missing four days of school, but I told him that someday his brother would want to know what it had been like when we brought him home, and Jon would be able to tell him what he remembered. Jon decided to go with us. We drove from Nebraska to Mississippi in two days, staying overnight in St. Louis.

After we checked into the Super 8 in Tupelo, I paged Debbie, who called us immediately. She told us that she would call the cradle care family, and they would bring the baby to our motel room. A few minutes later, Debbie and her husband arrived, followed by the cradle care parents and their youngest son (age thirteen), who was adopted. The cradle care mother, Gwen, carried Philip to me and placed him in my arms. I was in total shock—time stood still! We talked for a few minutes, and Gwen and her husband told us that Philip had been "projectile vomiting" and that he would only accept one kind of pacifier. Soon, everyone prepared to leave. Gwen said goodbye to Philip with tears in her eyes. After the others left, we were alone with our new baby. For the first time, we were a family of four instead of a family of three!

Tom held his new son and talked to him softly, and then Jonathan held his little brother and looked down at him. Suddenly Jon's face contorted and he began to cry. He had been an only child for eleven years, and suddenly he was an older brother. Life would never be the same again. It was a lot to absorb all at once. I changed Philip's diaper and was delighted to see that his little penis was still intact, not circumcised. In this way, he was just like his older brother. After a little while, Philip began to cry, and we thought he might be hungry. Tentatively, I filled the nursing supplementer bag with formula and held the tiny tube against my nipple, then brought Philip close to my breast. He looked puzzled for a split second, then latched on almost immediately and began to nurse as if he had been doing so since birth. I wondered if he was thinking, "What took you so long, Mom?" At that moment, I truly felt that Philip had accepted me as his mother. I felt a deep sense of joy and fulfillment. Here, at last, was the baby I had awaited for such a long time.

Philip slept between my husband and me that night in the motel, and Jon slept in the other double bed. Jon was not thrilled to have his sleep interrupted by the crying of his new brother. Philip snuggled next to me all night. At one point, when I got out of bed to warm another bag of formula, I felt a surge of panic. At forty, was I still up to the challenge of mothering a newborn baby? The panic subsided, and Philip and I went back to sleep.

We stayed in Tupelo for a couple of days until the court appearance when we officially became Philip's legal guardians. (Adoptions cannot be finalized until the baby has been with his new family for six months.) Right after we left the courtroom, we checked out of the motel and started the two-day drive back to Nebraska.

A couple of days after we got home, we took Philip to the pediatrician for a checkup. The doctor was worried about his weight. Philip had weighed six pounds, ten ounces at birth, and Gwen had told me that at his ten-day checkup he had weighed seven pounds. Now, at four weeks, he weighed only six pounds, thirteen ounces—he had lost some weight. I recalled the "projectile vomiting" mentioned by Gwen and her husband. Philip also had eczema. His skin was dry and wrinkled easily. The pediatrician asked us to come back daily for a week so she could monitor his weight gain. We found that he was gaining an ounce a day, and his skin gradually began to look smooth and moist.

I did not take any medications to induce nursing, but I did take a couple of fenugreek capsules with each meal. It was not obvious to me exactly when I began producing milk—there was no dramatic "let-down" of milk all at once, as I had experienced after giving birth to Jonathan. However, I soon began to feel a let-down sensation shortly after beginning each nursing session. To be on the safe side, I kept using the Lact-Aid supplementer for several months as Philip gradually took less and less formula and continued to grow at a steady rate. Finally, when he was about eight months old, we had returned from a trip to Chicago. I was exhausted after the long car trip and too tired to prepare a bag of formula. I sat down in my desk chair to nurse Philip, and I noticed that milk was dripping from my other breast. After that revelation, I discontinued the formula altogether. He was eating solids at that point, and clearly I was producing plenty of milk. It was so wonderful to be able to simply reach over and put Philip to my breast when he woke at night, instead of getting out of bed to warm up a bag of formula.

Now it is May 2002, and Philip is three and a half years old, healthy and happy. Like his older brother, he is bright, talkative, and full of energy. He still sleeps between my husband and me in our king-sized bed. He nurses a little in the morning after the alarm goes off, but the rest of the day he gets along fine without "bah-boos" (the code word we invented for nursing when Jonathan was a toddler). Philip has a close and loving relationship with my mother, who helped take care of him when he was younger. For more than two years, he took his daily naps in Grandma's arms so I could work in my home office. Philip brought sunshine to my father's life as his health failed during the final years of his life, and he helped distract my mother from the sense of helplessness she felt as my father slowly, inexorably faded away and then left us. (Dad died in February 2001.)

Philip and Jonathan have a loving, tempestuous relationship, like any two brothers. Philip loves to tease Big Brother, and he tries to get attention any way he can, whether it is positive or negative. Jonathan gets annoyed with Philip's antics but still feels protective and proud of him. One time he told me that if anyone ever made a racist comment around Philip, they'd better watch out for his Big Brother! Yesterday, without being asked to do so, Jon cut his little brother's fingernails when he noticed that they were getting long. Phil loves his Daddy dearly, even though he gleefully proclaims, "I love Mommy best!" (That is, when he's not telling me I'm a "poop head" for refusing to give him something he wants). He plays with Daddy and gets "under-ducks" on the swings at the park, and he nestles close to Daddy at night when it's time to go to sleep. Daddy goes to bed early with Philip so I can get a couple of hours of work done while everyone else is asleep. In the morning, Philip and I get out of bed after Tom and Jon have left for work and school. After we wake up and have breakfast, Phil goes to day care from 9:30 a.m. to 3:15 p.m. while I work. (We could not survive financially without my income.) Phil began going to daycare two months before his third birthday. He plays well with the other children and is the best "eater" in the group. He gets a sticker every day for eating all of his lunch. Phil's best friend is Justice, who is also black and has two loving white parents who, coincidentally, also have a family bed.

Yes, attachment parenting is possible with an adopted child. I am so closely attached to Philip that one night I had a dream in which I was trying to remember details of my pregnancy with him. I woke up and remembered that I had not carried him in my womb, but "only" in my heart. I feel blessed to be his mother.

Janet Tilden *lives in Omaha, Nebraska with her husband and two sons. She is grateful for what she has learned from both of her sons, who taught her how to give them whatever they needed. She is still learning every day!*

A Weaning Story
Notes from a Work in Progress
Bonnie Adams

As I nursed my firstborn of six months, I contemplated how much he had grown and how quickly the time had already passed. I tearfully mourned the loss of his early infancy. The big milestone on my mind was weaning. According to the books, the in-laws, and the neighbors, it was time. Conventional wisdom held that any mother who nursed past six months was some kind of sicko who was meeting her own, vaguely sexual, needs by forcing this poor innocent to breastfeed. It was time to get a bottle and a babysitter and let go. I cradled him and thought about weaning. I was full of guilt and completely unprepared for the depth of my pain at the mere thought of ending our nursing relationship. Charlie had taken to breastfeeding easily and completely. From the very beginning he was in love with the breast, the milk, and the sucking. There was nothing this child didn't adore about nursing. His cries were readily answered; his total bliss evident to all. How could I even consider taking this from him when it was so important, such a vital part of his rather limited world?

As you may have guessed, I couldn't do it. Not only that, I couldn't even try. With hormones coursing through my veins, I tearfully promised this precious child that I would never be the agent of his weaning. That step would belong to him. The very thought of depriving him of breastfeeding struck at the core of my new-mommy emotions. Sobbing aloud, I pledged to him that I would allow him his own course. My milk would always be available for him.

151

By the time Charlie was two, still obviously delighting in prolonged and frequent breastfeeding, I was pregnant again. I was so nauseous and tired that I attempted to wean him at night. The attempt resulted in misery for both of us. I got less sleep than I ever had and Charlie began to have temper tantrums during the day. After a few days of this unhappiness, I gathered my bewildered little boy into my arms. Rocking him and weeping (oh, those hormones!), I recommitted to allowing him to wean in his own time, trusting that he would let me know when he was ready to let go.

My second son, Jack, was born at thirty-one weeks' gestation and spent his first weeks in the Neonatal ICU. For some of that time, he was unable to nurse at all. I pumped my breasts until the hospital freezer was full. The staff wanted to "wean" him to formula in order to control his jaundice. I refused. Sitting by his incubator, both of us entangled in tubes and wires, I caressed him and promised this impossibly small bundle the same things I had promised his brother. "Breast is best," and he would have the best, anywhere, anytime, for as long as he needed it. The milk was here for him. He and only he would decide when to give it up.

This has not always been an easy promise to keep. There are many economic, cultural, and private forces conspiring in ways both overt and covert to separate mothers from their babies. I have received enough criticism to force me to look carefully at my decision to follow child-led weaning. I owe it to Charlie and Jack to do what is best for them regardless of how uncomfortable it may or may not make me or those around me. So, no apologies to the woman in the park who gave me such a disapproving look, or to the relatives who mutter under their breath. No expert in the world knows more than I do about this child, on this day, at this park. You move from, "Watch the baby, not the clock," to, "Listen to the child, not the neighbors." It's all the same wisdom. When it comes to raising children, our culture has much to say, our relatives have much to say, our hearts have much to say, and our children have much to say. We have to decide who we're going to listen to.

As for me, I'll listen to my heart and my son. The word "weaning" entered his vocabulary when he was about four. When I explained what the term meant, he burst into tears. The idea of there being an end to nursing had never occurred to him.

"Mommy, I would be so sad if I couldn't nurse!" He refused to believe that his feelings might someday change. I told him of my promise.

"In our family the children decide when they are ready to wean."

"Then I'll nurse until I'm a grown-up," he declared. Clearly, this child was not ready.

My son Jack was a very different kind of nurser. He could not take solids and was breastfed exclusively for fourteen months. Even so, he never really seemed to care for nursing. It was his only food, yet Jack could take it or leave it. This was strange for me, because my other son was still nursing avidly. The joke at our house became that Jack was going to wean before Charlie. Okay, I thought, as long as it is Jack's decision. His neutral attitude towards nursing provided me with an interesting defense to those who thought that his brother Charlie was nursing on my demand, for my needs, or that I had somehow made him into a child that needed to nurse for such a long time. Since Jack was so different, it would seem that Charlie's nursing style was more about Charlie and his needs, not the way he was being parented. I felt vindicated.

A wise mother once advised me that, like the pears in the produce department, developing children are "ripe when they yield to gentle pressure." Time and again I have found this to be true. A little push in the general direction of, say, potty training, has always provided me with irrefutable evidence of whether or not my child was "ripe." Respecting their readiness has led to several stops and starts as my "gentle pressure" has sometimes proved to be ill-timed. When I was off base, my boys have always let me know. When the timing was right, it all fell into place almost effortlessly. Thus they have started solids, rolled over, crawled, walked, started preschool, and even night-weaned, each according to his own internal pace.

Jack recently turned three. He nurses about twice a day.
When he is hurt, he would rather cuddle. When he is thirsty he
prefers orange juice. He still needs to nurse in order to relax
enough to fall asleep. There's no telling how long this will go on,
but I don't foresee him weaning in the near future. Charlie is five
and a half now. He nurses just once daily, as part of his bedtime
routine. His need seems to have changed again. His nursing
seems more of a wonderful habit. I used to think that I had given
birth to the first child in human history who would not wean.
Now, however, I can see his weaning on the horizon. Maybe a
few months from now, maybe a year, but he is surely "winding
down."

My boys and I have moved together from demand feedings,
toddlers tugging at my shirt, and public tandem "events" into a
much more sedate, private, and low-key personal ritual. Both of
my children sleep through the night (well, maybe not every
night!), neither of them nurses in public anymore (really, it just
doesn't come up!), and I can't remember the last time I nursed
two simultaneously. In the past six months, Charlie has actually
skipped a few days. (Eight times. I keep track.) Even Jack has
done that once. Clearly we have moved into a new phase of our
nursing relationships.

When my babies were new, the thought of them weaning
nearly broke my heart. As they grew, I must confess that there
were days when I dreaded their requests to nurse and wished
they would just wean already. Even at those times, however, I
could not actually picture mothering without nursing. If you
cannot offer a breast, what do you actually do when they're hurt,
tired, hungry, frightened, or about to have a tantrum? I often felt
that I'd have no idea how to be a parent if I couldn't nurse. As
time has gone on and my children's need to nurse has changed
and diminished, we have, of course, developed other ways to
address their daily needs.

As my oldest heads to kindergarten and my youngest faces
potty training, it is time for me to accept that their needs will
change again. We are heading out of this intensive "hands-on"
toddler stage of mothering. I am so excited to see what the future
holds for us. One aspect of it will no doubt include a couple of

weanings in the coming months or years. I cannot promise that I won't shed a tear, but I am confident that it will not be the hormonal outpouring of several years ago. Weaning now looks to me as if it will be as natural and easy as some of the other milestones have turned out to be.

We are more ready now than we have ever been. Some time, probably soon, my child will signal that he is readier still and the time will have come. I plan to take his hand and, perhaps wistfully, follow his sure and steady lead into the next stage.

Bonnie Adams *lives in New Jersey with her husband, Jim, and longtime nurslings Charlie and Jack.*

NURSING THROUGH ADVERSITY
Christi Colvin

My son is now five months old and breastfeeds like a champ, but I can remember feeling that we would never get the hang of it just a few short months ago; I would be doomed to pump forever. I never realized how every little thing that happens during the birth of a child can affect his ability to breastfeed. I was induced three weeks early, given Pitocin, Stadol, and an epidural, and Ryland was delivered with the assistance of a vacuum due to a drop in his heart rate. He was also a little slow to breathe. All of this, combined with his severe jaundice, set the stage for a very long road to breastfeeding.

My milk didn't come in until day five, and the nurses in the hospital, although they were all supposed to be lactation consultants, offered no help. Ryland quickly became jaundiced after we took him home, and I was pressured by the pediatricians to give him formula to help "push the bilirubin through his system more quickly." So I did. My husband and I would alternate every other bottle with formula and pumped breast milk. Finally, we got rid of the jaundice, but I still couldn't get him to latch on and nurse. He would arch his back and scream, and I would cry and feel like a failure. I kept thinking that no one ever told me how difficult it would be! I remember sitting in bed pumping every hour (with a hand pump) around the clock and crying. So many times I was ready to give up, but I really wanted to nurse my son.

Finally, after two weeks, I found a La Leche League meeting nearby and off we went. The ladies were so great; they helped me latch him, and he actually breastfed. I was thrilled. I tried again when we got home, and when he nursed once again, I thought we were finally set. And then he went back to the arching and screaming. Two weeks after that, I scheduled an appointment with a lactation consultant and had a three-hour meeting with her. She informed me that an epidural can affect a baby for up to two months, if not longer, after birth. She taught me how to use a nipple shield, helped me latch him, introduced me to Mother's Milk tea, and finally got us on the right track. I left there feeling better than I had since he'd been born. We still had problems, but we were nursing. Ryland was still fussy, but I started to notice it was only right after eating. And he was still arching his back and crying. Finally I got on the Internet and started reading some articles on Dr. Sears' website about reflux. Ryland fit the profile exactly, so I made an appointment with our pediatrician and took him in. We started Ryland on Zantac and saw immediate results.

When Ryland was about three months old, I did away with the nipple shield and he's been breastfeeding ever since. Actually, he won't even take a bottle now! After everything I went through trying to nurse him, I can't think of a bigger compliment from my son. Although it would be nice to leave him for more than two hours at a time, I think back to when I was pumping while my husband bottle-fed him, and I know how blessed I am to have made it this far. I pretty much went through hell to be able to nurse him, but I wouldn't have had it any other way. Breastfeeding just feels so right; I can honestly say I would have done whatever it took to be able to give this gift to my son. For, by doing so, I am also giving a gift to myself. I look at my chunky little man and feel such an enormous degree of accomplishment. Not only was I able to carry him and bring him into this world, but my milk put those rolls on his little legs. Breastfeeding is the most rewarding thing I have ever done and I am infinitely glad that I was so determined. It has all been worth it in the end.

Christi Colvin is a WAHM with one beautiful son (for now) and a wonderful husband. She is also "webmom" to a site that allows moms to market and sell their products without the hassle of running a website. Visit www.CraftyMommy.com for more information.

No Num Nums...No Book!

Jeanne Holden

Cameron wakes up at 6:05 as he does every morning. His sister, Maura, wakes up as well. It is almost as if the sun whispered in both of their ears that the sky was lit up. As usual, Mommy comes into Cameron's room to give him a big kiss and open his blinds, to affirm the presence of the beautiful day. Together, Mommy and Cameron go into Maura's room to say "hi." Maura jumps and screeches with excitement as Mommy reaches for her. Cameron chats with Maura, letting her know that he, like Mommy, loves her very much.

Mommy changes Maura in to her play clothes, and Cameron, like a big boy, puts on his clothes all by himself. After he is done he very proudly walks into Maura's room and says, "All done, Mommy."

"Well, aren't you a big boy," says Mommy, "And you are very handsome." Cameron smiles, knowing that what Mommy said was true. Dressed and ready, the three make it to the kitchen to have breakfast. Cameron and Maura each have cereal, but Mommy makes it differently for the two. Cameron has cereal with store-bought milk and Maura had cereal with Num Nums.

Num Nums is what Mommy calls the milk that babies get when they are too little for the store kind. Mommy explained to Cameron that he called it Num Nums when he was a baby, so Mommy called it that, too.

First, Maura eats her cereal with Cameron and then Mommy picks her up and give her Num Nums. Sometimes Cameron would get mad and shout, "No Num Nums." Mommy would ask him to come over and sit with her and Maura to let him know he was special, too. Sometimes it's easy to feel left out, but Mommy always tries to make sure that Cameron knows how very special he is and that he can sit with her and Maura during Num Nums time or any time.

After breakfast and Num Nums time Cameron begins getting ready for school. Mommy packs his lunch, helps put on socks and shoes, and hooks on his backpack. All three of them sit on the front porch waiting for the school bus. Cameron looks around, feeling happy. It feels nice to have Mommy and Maura with him on the steps. He likes waking up at the same time as Maura, getting dressed with her, and eating cereal with her. He doesn't have Num Nums like her, but that's because he's bigger and can eat things that she can't.

"I love you, Mommy, I love you, Maura," says Cameron.

"We love you, too, Cameron," said Mommy. Cameron smiles, feeling happy inside.

The bus comes, and Cameron climbs aboard and waves as he rides away to school. Mommy and Maura go inside after they wave goodbye, and play for a while. Before they know it, the bus screeches in front of the house and Cameron comes running out.

"Mommy, Maura, I'm home," he shouts.

"Hi, sweetie, how was your day?"

"Very good, I played and sang and counted and read." Maura grabs her brother for a hug. He is happy to be home with his mommy and sister.

Cameron and Maura each have some crackers and drink for snack, but Maura's drink is different. After her crackers, Mommy gives her Num Nums, like she did in the morning. Before giving Maura her Num Nums, she walks Cameron to his room for his nap and tucks him in bed. Mommy and Maura read him his favorite dinosaur book and give him a kiss. Unhappy about what is coming, Cameron shouts, "No Num Nums, no book."

"Cameron," Mommy says quietly, "Maura likes a drink and a book, too. You know that Mommy and Maura love you, don't you?" Cameron nods and puts his head down. He knows that Mommy loves him; he just felt sad when Maura was getting Num Nums and he wasn't.

Mommy and Maura leave Cameron's room and shut the door. Some time passes, and Maura's door begins to open ever so gently. Behind the door is Cameron, walking on his tippy toes. Mommy calls him over quietly to sit with Maura and her. All together, Mommy, Maura, and Cameron read a book. Mommy rocks and reads until both children are asleep.

Mommy tucks Maura and Cameron in bed, and as she is about to close Cameron's door, she hears a voice say, "Mommy, I know I can't have Num Nums like Maura, but I sure like the book."

Mommy smiles. "Me too, sweetie, sweet dreams."

※ ※ ※ ※ ※

The end.

Jeanne Holden is a stay-at-home mom and writer who resides in Chesapeake, Virginia with her husband, Scott, five-year-old son, Cameron, and two-year-old daughter, Maura. She breastfed both of her children and is very happy with their decision to keep Cameron intact. Her children have inspired her to write children's books.

BABY WEARING

Oh, Baby, the Places We'll Go... In Our Sling!

Christine Jones Regan

I love my sling! Of all the baby "paraphernalia" we bought before and immediately after my daughter was born, the sling has become our most prized possession. While other "must have" items sit around collecting dust, our sling collects memories.

My first glimpse of a mom wearing her baby in a sling was at a local store many years ago. I had no idea what it was at the time, except that it looked very interesting. I've always remembered that image of a loving mom holding her baby close to her heart.

I am one of those women who likes to be prepared, very prepared. Early on, I knew I would want to have my baby with me wherever we went. By the time I attended my first La Leche League meeting around my fifth month of pregnancy, my husband and I had already purchased one Snugli "sling" and one front-pack carrier.

At the meeting I saw several women all wearing their babies in the same type of "carrier" that I had seen on the mom in the store many years earlier. I watched with great admiration how these moms held and cradled their babies with ease in such a natural-looking way. By the meeting's end I just had to ask exactly what was this great invention and where could I get one. It was then that a mom put me in touch with her doula, who was also an Over the Shoulder Baby Holder distributor. I e-mailed her right after the meeting. We met over a cup of tea, and she had me sold on the many benefits of slinging within minutes. She also warned me that the need for our Snuglis would become obsolete—and we learned soon enough that she was right.

At first I was a little nervous about putting my tiny baby girl in our sling, so I first tried her in the so-called Snugli "sling." It had straps, buckles, and snaps, and was stiff as a board. The baby could only lie horizontally in it, and it was a sweat factory. I knew this wasn't going to work. Then I tried her in the sling. "Ahh...Now this is more like it," I said. I could feel her tiny body close to mine. I could wrap my arms around her without any buckles or a bulky board getting in the way. I put my Snugli into a drawer, never to be used again.

This wasn't to say that everything was smooth sailing immediately thereafter. It took some time for me to gain confidence in my slinging abilities. At first, Aisling cried every time I put her in for more than a few minutes. And I was never quite sure if I had her in correctly. A few pep talks from my doula friend and some practice took care of that. Even now, she still prefers to be in it when she goes out of the house, in full motion in her sling, so I'm not exactly vacuuming, cooking, and making the beds with her in it. Err, okay, to be honest I'm not doing any of those things anyway!

❋ ❋ ❋ ❋ ❋

I could write about all the many advantages of slinging for both mother and baby, but most of you know those already. What I do love talking about is how indispensable our sling has become. There hasn't been any place that we can't go together in it yet. In fact, it has become my personal challenge to see just how many fun places we can sling in.

Let's talk about convenience. I have to admit, I'm a weakling. Just thinking about pulling out a stroller from the trunk or lugging a car seat around makes me break into a sweat. When we go out, I just put on my sling, put the baby in, and off we go. I've never had to worry about whether or not we'd fit through a store aisle or through a crowded restaurant.

Versatility? One of our first solo excursions sans Daddy was to the toy store. Aisling hung out in the sling, tummy-to-tummy with Mommy, and nursed while I pushed the shopping cart. I was so excited that I called my doula friend up from the car to tell her that we walked through the store and checkout nursing the whole time with no one the wiser. On the other hand, my husband is not so happy that I can now easily carry a backpack and five bulging shopping bags of more baby "stuff" through the mall, to and from the car, and up three flights of stairs with Aisling in my arms.

While many parents gripe about what a hassle it is to travel with young babies, my husband and I have found the exact opposite to be true. My little girl is almost six months old, and we've been everywhere together, thanks to the sling.

Restaurants? No problem! Our favorite place to go with Grand Pop is an all-you-can-eat buffet. Aisling sits up and peers out while Mommy gets her food, then we slide into a booth, and if baby gets tired, Mommy lays her down in the sling and she nurses to sleep while Mommy and Daddy enjoy the rest of their meal. I love to see the looks on people's faces when they ask if they can hold my baby while I eat, only to find out that she is actually having her meal at the same time.

Weddings? No problem! At an outdoor wedding, the mother of the bride came up to us to see if we really had a baby with us because someone had told her we did—but she hadn't heard anything the entire time. Aisling had been quietly observing most of the time in her sling.

Getting a haircut? No problem! Normally, I'd only schedule appointments on the weekend, when my hubby could go with me. However, one day I felt I had to get it all chopped off, so I made a last-minute appointment. Mommy got her hair washed, cut, and styled with baby nursing and sleeping in the sling. (By the way, notice a pattern regarding sleeping? Slinging is a great way to soothe your baby to sleep, especially if they are overstimulated.)

Sporting events? No problem. Aisling took her Daddy out to a minor league baseball game for his first Father's Day present. We sat on the lawn by the outfield, nursed and napped on a big blanket, and slept right through fireworks, snuggled safely in our

sling. She didn't hear a thing with the soft cushioned sides pulled
up around her ears.

How about museums, churches, and parks? Trains and cabs?
Or hikes and walks in the city? We've even proudly marched in
the La Leche World Walk for Breastfeeding with a large wooden
sign in hand. Well, you get the picture. I feel so much more *secure*
with baby on me. And speaking of "security," my second admis-
sion is that I'm a big klutz. A feature I happen to really like about
the sling I use is the extra padding in the shoulders and on the
sides. Once or twice I've been known to walk into a wall or slip
over a banana peel, and the padding comes in handy.

Everywhere we go, we seem to generate a lot of attention,
especially from moms struggling with a toddler on one hip and
pushing a cart or stroller with the other hand. Many think that
their babies are too big for a sling, but I tell them otherwise.
Some ask, "Is the baby really comfortable all squished up in there
like that?" Yes. But the best is when nice people come up to comment on how comfy she looks. Once, a grandfatherly man asked
me if he could "jump in there" and fall asleep, too. One of my
recent favorites is, "Oh she looks so cozy in there, peeking out
just like a little baby kangaroo!" People can see how content she
is, and this has helped us meet people that might not have come
up to us otherwise. In talking to other moms about my sling,
sometimes we also get around to discussing natural birth, breastfeeding, and attachment parenting. Slinging has brought so
much positive energy into our lives that I recently decided to
become a distributor myself. It's just another wonderful way for
my daughter and me to do more together.

Now that my *baby* girl is getting bigger, we'll probably start
to hang her feet out the bottom, and later, we'll use the hip-
carry. Sure, I know that one day she will be too big for her sling
and I'll be running to keep up with her, but I hope that she will
remember the bonds we formed while slinging, and will always
be running back to my arms. Luckily for Mommy, we've got
quite some time before that day comes.

In closing, try going out without your sling once you get
used to it. Slinging makes simple trips to the post office or even
the mailbox easier. I won't be caught without mine now, as

evidenced by the extra sling in the car and one at Pop's. And guess who else has his own sling now too? That's right, Daddy! So what became of his Snugli, you ask? It never really made it out of the drawer. We're a one hundred percent complete slinging family now, and we wouldn't have it any other way.

Christine Jones Regan *and husband Brian share a family bed with their daughter, Aisling, and three cats (yes, three) in West Orange, New Jersey. Aisling is their first child. She was born gently into the world via natural birth in April 2002 at New Jersey's only remaining freestanding birth center. In her previous lives (before becoming a proud SAHM mom), Christine was a book events manager and a women and children's advocate at a domestic violence agency. She is now a lactation educator/counselor and an Attachment Parenting International support group leader, and she is currently completing her postpartum doula certification. She is also an adopted Korean who writes and speaks about transcultural adoption issues. In their "spare time," Christine and Aisling also have fun "pretending" to work together as mommy and baby nursing models. Mommy, Daddy, and the little toddling one are still happily "slinging along" together!*

TRUE LOVE AND THE RIGHT ACCESSORIES

Sue Landsman

When we were expecting our first child, likely a boy, we did the whole traditional expecting thing—the nursery painted butter yellow with a jungle wallpaper border, the crib set up nicely with the light blue and stars sheet pattern, ready and waiting for the baby. Then he came and our new world began, completely unlike what we had expected. From day one, he slept in our bed, along with our seventy-pound dog, our arms splayed out beside him like the cutest totem pole. The bassinet remained full of laundry. Soon, after learning to nurse lying down, I wouldn't even remember in the morning when and how often I'd nursed him at night. I woke up to smiles, warm little feet tucked next to my legs, and the heavenly smell of warm, milky baby skin.

Three months later, we walked into the nursery, and noticed an odd, oily, oval black spot at one end of the crib. Apparently the cat had been enjoying it. The bassinet was now completely submerged in laundry. The swing and the bouncy seat went unappreciated—like the cats, our son was a connoisseur of human warmth, and just wanted to be on someone all the time. I bought a sling and carried him around everywhere. He slept with us until he was about a year and a half old, when my husband started getting tired of the family bed idea. Then my husband slept with him in another room, while I slept alone with the dog.

After the second child, a daughter, our baby items got better use. The crib helped prop things up in the basement, and my son spent many happy hours teaching his toys how to vibrate in the bouncy seat. My $14-a-pair natural-wool breast pads became the crucial prop in the "let's see how long the cat can keep this on his back" game. I bought two more slings. She slept with us for about a year. Then my husband slept with both kids in another room while I slept alone with the dog.

With the third child, we truly learned the meaning of "kangaroo care." Now, with no actual baby items other than diapers anywhere in the house, the baby is just a slightly-higher-bulge-than-before in the fleece pouch in front of Mommy. I always know when he needs to nurse, because as soon as he makes a sound my daughter will shriek, "Baby's crying! He needs ingie!" Oddly, she's not at all interested in nursing or tending to her dolls, but she simply must carry around the "nipple cream," because it comes in that fab purple container and fits in her tiny purses. I've bought two more slings and lent one to a friend. This baby will sleep with us, undoubtedly, until he joins the somewhat puzzling "everyone-except-Mommy" bed and I resume my intimate relationship with the dog.

As the children get bigger, it's becoming harder to both feel and convey the adoration that the close body warmth and endless kisses of their early years made so easy. I miss the days when we just rocked together, or all I had to do was tilt my face down to kiss their little heads. We would grin foolishly at each other, in our own little world, sharing a secret that all the moms and babies separated by strollers and hallways were missing out on.

Now I find myself focusing less on this simple giving than on how well they're meeting my behavioral expectations, or how close they are to pissing me off to the point of screaming at them. Their arms and legs have gotten long and lanky, and their bodies and minds move quicker than mine. It's hard to remember they're still little. We spend too much time at odds with each other, frustration and bad feelings stuck in the air like the scent of old fish. Sometimes I think we just need to crawl back into bed together, quiet and still, until we can once again pay attention to what nourished us both when they were babies. That is, after all, how I wanted to parent. The best thing we can give our children is trust—trust that they won't take advantage of us, that they won't go bad from too much love, that we can live together in a place where we can give freely and have our needs met without asking.

But of course, nobody notices when things go right. Love, properly, is like air—sweet and invisible. As long as nobody poops in the bed.

Sue Landsman is the mother of three. She is a natural childbirth educator and sling geek, and is currently enjoying homeschooling her two older children and nursing her third.

IT'S A SLING THING
Tiffany Palisi

The first time I saw a sling was at a La Leche League meeting. I was holding my then sixteen-pound son in my very tired arms and wondered if the hippie-like contraption was worth a shot.

My son was about six weeks old and we had already, unsuccessfully, tried using a front carrier. If you've never used a front carrier, let me explain. It is this complex padded thing with lots of ins and outs for a baby's arms, legs, and head. Very confusing. Our problems all began while I first tried to figure out the snaps and straps. My son started to cry in my arms so my husband, Johnny, held and rocked him for a bit, and then, after minutes of my trying to work the front carrier and failing, my husband took over and passed my son to me. Johnny got everything in order and laid the front carrier, just so, on the couch. He took our son back in his arms and told me to slide the carrier over my arms without moving anything else or he'd have to readjust everything. I got it on but couldn't get my son's legs through the straps properly. Again, my husband and I worked as a team to get him into it. When we finally did, all I kept thinking was that his testicles were being crushed. He was screaming, I was crying. I frantically asked my husband to help undo the stupid thing, which really irked him since he'd just paid $85 for it.

So when I checked out the sling, I immediately thought about the trouble it would be to get my son in it and figure out how to work it. Throughout the meeting, I saw two mothers actively using their slings. One mom had a toddler in hers; the toddler would ride in the sling for a while and then, when she wanted to explore she would easily be released into the welcoming group of mothers and children. Later, when she wished to

175

nurse she approached her mother, who'd spent most of the meeting standing, and asked, "Nuss?" Her mother picked her up, put her in the sling and began nursing. She made it look so easy. The other mother had her four-month-old daughter in her sling. This mother sat for most of the meeting and looked pretty comfortable. Her child was sleeping soundly while she ate a bagel, drank some juice, and chatted. She had both hands free while her child was just inches from her heart.

After the meeting I spoke separately to each of the mothers to ask them about their slings. They each told me how they could easily get things done around the house with their children "on board" and loved the fact that their babies were so close to them. Both were using the same brand and raved about the sling's ease of use. It cost just over $30, so I thought it was worth a try.

On my ride home, I thought about the joy these mothers had. Their babies were always so close to them, listening to adult conversations and watching people talk. They were learning how people communicate. Further, because they were upright, bending when mom did and turning when mom did, they were getting their vestibular apparatus stimulated, which would later help with balance when they would learn to crawl and walk. It all made sense. But it looked so *sixties*.

I went home and told my husband about the Mayan-inspired slings. He looked at me, laughed, and said, "Oh yeah, it'll be just like the Baby Bjorn. It'll sit in a ball somewhere until you find the time to return it." Actually, I had about as much faith in my ability to use the sling as he did, but I was feeling desperate. So I called the 800 number and ordered the sling. Instead of choosing a colorful paisley or tie-dyed pattern (God forbid), I requested black. The woman explained that the black slings were on backorder for three weeks. Since three weeks would be three weeks too long, she suggested I go with an undyed fabric (think pale wheat). And that's what I did.

Three days later, my sling arrived. It was in one straight piece—a long, thick gathering of fabric with two brass rings on one end. I immediately regretted buying it. It looked nothing like the little hammocks the mothers at the LLL meeting had worn. I began to get flustered and quickly scrambled for the instruction manual. It was nothing more than a sheet of paper with a person holding a baby in a sling and arrows telling me, the reader, exactly what to do. I am not very good with instructions (just ask my mom), and so, after a horrifying IKEA flashback, I plunged back into the box in search for more help.

By the Grace of God, I discovered a how-to video tucked in the bottom of the box. I popped it into my VCR with the hope of finding the answer to slinging my son. While it was very helpful, and I was able to get the sling on and my baby in without any help (Bravo!), I felt as though he was getting lost in the sling. Was I doing something wrong?

I called Liz, one of the two sling-wearers I'd met at the LLL meeting. She wasn't home, so I left a long, detailed list of questions on her answering machine. When she finally called me back hours later, she offered me the gift of a lifetime: a personal visit to my house to help me with my sling.

It was a few days before Liz arrived, and each day I'd try to put my son in the sling. I was able to get him in, but I felt that he was slipping out of the bottom. So I'd hold onto his rear end the whole time he was in the sling, concerned that he'd drop out the bottom. I would have canned the sling entirely, were it not for Liz. She explained that I had pulled the fabric through improperly, preventing the sling from allowing the weight of the baby to be countered by the tail of the sling. I'd also had the two rings at nipple level when they really should have been sitting just below my shoulder. She tweaked my technique and got my son and me slinging.

At first, I felt embarrassed by wearing my sling. It seemed I was the only person outside of the LLL meetings using my sling. I'd go to the mall, the bookstore, or a restaurant and people would stare, or at least I thought they did. I wondered if they thought I was "crunchy" (I am) and if they judged my ability to mother my child based on the fact that he wasn't in a stroller. It seemed all the other babies I saw were in some form of plastic equipment (stroller, car seat, highchair). People inside our social circle asked why we were opposed to using our brand new stroller. I explained that we had tried it once but it was awful. The baby was so far away, at eye level with cigarettes held by passersby, and always looking at people's knees. Outside, bugs flew at his face and the sun's rays blinded him. In the sling, he was safe and content. He could block out the sun by burrowing his nose into my shoulder. I could always see what he was doing, and would quickly notice if he was uncomfortable. Best of all, I could nurse him without anyone even knowing.

When I'd go grocery shopping, I'd never have to worry about the cart tipping with him in it or be concerned about someone taking him because he'd be in the sling, attached to me. And when I went into the cold sections of the store, I'd drape the tail of the sling around his neck and over his head to keep him from getting a chill.

People everywhere warned that I'd spoil him, or that by carrying him "so much" I'd prevent him from learning to crawl or walk. The fact is that since he was always upright, he had no problem holding up his head. He both sat up and walked at around the same time that most of his peers did. And he was walking, without holding onto anything, at eleven months. Clearly, sling wearing did not cause a problem with gross motor functions.

"But what if you fall?" someone asked with a trace of concern. At that point, I had already fallen with my son in the sling, down four steps, actually. My mother was in the house with me, and as I began to fall I vividly remember calling out to my mom, "I'm falling!" As I tumbled, everything went in slow motion. If you've ever had a car accident, you know what I mean. Thoughts of my son's head, bloodied and split open, ran through my mind. I envisioned the paramedics taking him away in an ambulance with my mother and me beside him. But somehow (my pediatrician calls it maternal instinct), I fell just beside him, cradling him tightly in the sling. We were both just fine.

You know, I cannot tell you how many times mothers have told me about incidents where their babies, while being held in the portable car seat/carrier have fallen out (after not being properly strapped in) or when the mother, unaware of just how close the car seat was to the wall/door/railing, smacked the seat/carrier right into something hard, thus injuring the baby. The way

I look at it, it's a whole lot safer wearing your baby on your body than pushing him in a stroller or carrying her in a car seat.

✳ ✳ ✳ ✳ ✳

It's been just over two years, and my son and I are still happily using our sling. We use our first one and have three more for backup. While he often prefers walking or running to riding in the sling, it is still useful. When we enter a new situation, he likes the safety of the sling. When he's tired of walking (like for four hours at the Bronx Zoo) he says, "Mama, sling please." Or at the supermarket when there are no "little carts" or racecar carts, he'll often opt for the sling. And of course, when he just wakes up from his nap he wants the closeness that the sling offers.

Rarely is a sling out of my reach. I keep one in the car at all times because we often use one while running errands. It's also great if I need to walk from store to store, because I don't have to worry about my son running into the street or getting lost. I know that, as he begins to grow and approach the forty-pound mark, the sling will be a thing of the past. For now, though, we enjoy every minute of behaving like kangaroos.

Tiffany Palisi is the proud mother of John Henry, who, at two and a half years old, loves co-sleeping, nursing, and riding in the sling. She functions as a NOCIRC center and loves educating people on natural attachment parenting.

THE CIRCUMCISION DECISION

WHY WE CHOSE NOT TO CIRCUMCISE

Jennifer E. Moore

I had never really thought about the foreskin, or lack of it, until I saw the twenty-week ultrasound that showed my husband, Andy, and I for the first time our son's penis. We had agreed to find out the sex of our child if possible, and were overjoyed that he complied by generously opening his legs for us (and the ultrasound tech) to see his "bits and pieces" in full view. While pregnant, I had the luxury of not having a job (other than growing our son in my ever-expanding belly), so I had lots of free time to learn about all sorts of choices I would have to make as the future mother of a baby boy, who we would name "Sebastian Elihu."

A message board for pregnant moms had a discussion going about circumcision, and whether you were "for it" or "against it" and why. All the male members of my immediate and extended family are circumcised (I found this out when we chose not to circumcise our son), and my husband came from a similar situation in his family. I searched for websites that talked about circumcision and gave the lowdown on how and why the procedure is performed in America. I learned, for instance, that we are the only country that routinely circumcises non-Jewish infant males.

Upon researching pro- and anti-circumcision arguments, I deemed circumcision unnecessary, and told Andy, my husband, about my findings. He was very understanding as we talked about reasons one would circumcise (e.g., Judaic tradition, wanting a son to "look like everyone else," etc.), and we agreed that none of these reasons would warrant this procedure to be performed on our son.

Andy and I didn't tell anyone about our choice (why should we?) until after Sebastian ("Seb") was born and they saw for themselves. My father, a dermatologist, had doubts, since he claimed to see "clean men," as he put it, come into his practice with problems stemming from an intact penis.

On a similar note, the comment we heard the most was, "That is so dirty, how will you keep it (his penis) clean?" Sadly, most people, even the highly educated, don't know that a foreskin doesn't even retract until a male is between two and four years of age, therefore, there is nothing to "keep clean." By the time Seb's foreskin retracts, he will be of an age when we can instruct him on the proper cleaning of his penis, which does not take much effort.

Another argument for circumcision is from fellow Christians who claim that it is scriptural to circumcise. Yes it is scriptural, but in the Old Testament Jewish faith. In the New Testament, numerous times it said that a man no longer needs outward circumcision in order to signify his relationship with God. Being Christians, we are believers in the New Testament.

I think the cultural norm of circumcising baby boys is probably why most people make this choice without even second-guessing why. The baby's dad is probably circumcised, so why not circumcise the child too? To this I say, "Does your child have his father's hair color? Exact body-build? Exact facial structure or eye color? Then why do you think his penis should look the same?" Also, I feel like asking the fathers who are pro-circumcision, "How often did you and your father or anyone else, for that matter, sit around and compare penises?"

Tampering with your child's body in this way is not our job, nor our right. If for some reason Seb wants to have his foreskin cut off when he is older, that is his right, the same as if he ever wants tattoos or body piercings. I have seen infant girls (and even a few boys) with pierced ears, and in the same vein, I wouldn't make that sort of choice for them, either.

With the choice of whether or not to circumcise, why act without researching it first, especially if the decision involves the permanent alteration of your child? I would rather make a choice because I fully believe that is the best possible decision I could make, not because it is simply the norm.

As parents, our children deserve the best, including the best-thought-out choices involving their upbringing and care. If Seb asks me someday, "Momma, why did/didn't you (insert parenting choice here)," I want to tell him, "Because your Daddy and I love you very much, and you are worth the time and effort it took to research and come to the decision to/not to (insert parenting choice here). Here are the reasons why."

Jennifer E. Moore *is the mother of one animal-loving toddler, Sebastian Elihu, and at the time of writing this article, is expecting child number two in early 2004. Jenn is married to her best friend, Andy, and lives in Central Pennsylvania. She is a stay-at-home mom who also enjoys tie-dying baby clothing. She attends her local La Leche League and MOPS (Mothers of Preschoolers), and in her spare time writes articles for her church newsletter. Jenn (and her husband, Andy) also enjoy discussing attachment parenting with family and friends.*

FOR THE LOVE OF PADDY

Bridget Willey

When I became pregnant with my son, I was thirty-one and had
known many women my age and younger who had gone
through horrible hospital birth experiences—epidurals they did-
n't want, impersonal care, C-sections that they discovered later
could have been prevented. I have a good friend whose marriage
was almost destroyed because she was given an episiotomy that
became infected and thickly scarred, preventing her from having
any semblance of a normal sex life. Her son is ten, and despite
several corrective procedures, she still has problems and experiences pain from regular medical checkups.

My own gynecologist, whom my mother used and who had
seen me since I was fourteen, refused to be my birth physician
because she thought I was crazy for not wanting to deliver in a
hospital and for stating, up front, that I did not want an epidural, an episiotomy, or any inducing drugs. She called me "an accident waiting to happen." Bear in mind that I have always been
healthy, am a non-smoker, and am athletic—there was no reason
to assume that I wouldn't be capable of a natural birth.

So, I went against the grain and chose to see a midwife for
my prenatal care and delivery. My midwife was wonderful, and
I knew I had found a great provider when she said, "Women
have been giving birth for millions of years. This is a life
process—not an illness—so I will treat you like a woman carrying a child, not a sick person." I had an uneventful pregnancy,
and no problems. My midwife told me that most pregnancy
issues—water retention, excess weight gain, toxemia, nausea,
etc.—are caused by poor nutrition and lifestyle/exercise habits.
She counseled me on how to eat for a healthy baby and body,

gave me books to read (Susan Weed and others), and told me to walk or get some moderate exercise daily. She also said that episiotomies are rarely, rarely needed if you have a skilled birth attendant who assists you in stretching properly, and that even if you tear, it will usually be minor and heal on its own.

I was afraid of giving birth, and again, my midwife said, "It's important not to have fear. Fear causes pain and causes your muscles not to work. Think of this as a marathon that your body was made to win. Work through the pain, and tell yourself that you can do this. The only way you won't be able to do this is if you convince yourself that you can't."

When I went into labor, I spent all of it at home, going to the birth center only when my water broke and was unable to sit because my son's head was crowning. My son was born fifteen minutes after we arrived at the birth center, I had no anesthesia whatsoever, and we went home in less than twelve hours. Was my birth painful? At times. But I kept telling myself that women all over the world do it every day. The best advice I got was to stay on my feet and pace the house or climb the steps (makes gravity work for you), and squat through painful contractions. Honestly, I have had menstrual cramps that were worse than my labor pain.

My son was a healthy six-and-a-half pounds, and he came out screaming and alert. Unlike a lot of women I know, I felt well enough after the birth to shower and eat, and the following day, I was doing laundry and cooking as I normally do. And, thanks to my midwife's nutrition suggestions, I have no stretch marks (I gained weight slowly and on good food, so my skin accommodated it) and was able to fit into my pre-pregnancy jeans less than a month after delivery, while at the same time being able to make enough milk to breastfeed my son.

I had already decided in my mind not to have my son circumcised, and my husband was a little taken aback during our initial consultation when the midwife told him that she did not do them on personal principle (he, like many people, assumed it was an automatic thing). If we chose to have it done, our son would need to be taken to the hospital and admitted, since it is not considered an outpatient operation. My husband backed down on the circumcision issue only when I showed him videos from the NOCIRC website. He was unaware of how painful and invasive they are, and he was shocked more when he learned that non-circumcised men are the exception rather than the rule in most parts of the world. Babies have died from circumcisions, which is also something he didn't know. My mother-in-law unwittingly helped as well by telling us how awful she felt when she had my husband and his brothers circumcised, because back in the '50s and '60s, circumcisions were automatic for hospital births. She said that she knew they were painful, didn't understand why they were done, and felt horrible because she didn't have a choice in the matter.

By the time my son was born, it had become a nonissue. As I told my husband and anyone else who asked me, "If he chooses to have it done when he is an older teen or a grown man, fine, but then it will be his choice and no one else's." Fortunately, we have a pediatrician whose personal view is that circumcision is largely an elective and is not medically necessary except in very rare cases. Our daycare provider had also said that she is seeing more and more intact boys—it's about fifty/fifty at this point—so my son is not unusual. So far, my son's being intact is no different than if he were circumcised.

In talking to other parents, the number one question that I hear is, "Isn't it hard to keep clean?" I always reply that an intact penis is as difficult to clean as your feet or any other part of your body. Soap and water—basic good hygiene—is really all that's needed. I'd spoken to other mothers of boys, and from what they tell me, the reverse is true: circumcised penises are messy and painful when they are healing, and the diaper rash and irritation is worse. At three and a half, my son already knows how to care for himself, and we have had no problems.

My son has noticed that there is a difference between how he looks and how his father looks (my son is learning to urinate standing, and he watches his father) and has asked about it, and we tell him the truth: that all bodies are unique and different, and that the way he looks is the way he was intended to look. I think that the explanation that you give has a lot to do with how your child and others view their intact state. It's no different than if I had a daughter with small breasts, or a child who was on the heavy side. It's critical that they learn to view themselves as "whole" just the way they are. Imagine how the cosmetic surgery industry (and I think of circs as a form of cosmetic surgery) would take a nose-dive if people were taught to accept themselves as-is!

Bridget Willey lives in Connecticut with her husband, John, and son, Patrick. Although making her living in the corporate world as a graphic artist, web designer, and marketing manager, she spends her free time studying herbal medicine, women's history/issues, and female-friendly pagan belief systems. She enjoys meeting (either in person or through the Internet) intelligent people who have positive and unique viewpoints and appreciates the opportunity to be a mother to a creative and wise child.

SAM

Donna M. Rucinski Harrington

Pregnant with our first child, my husband and I researched the circumcision issue. I learned that there was no medical reason for having the child circumcised. I did not want to circumcise, but eventually left the decision up to my husband, thinking it was a "guy thing." I could not have predicted the outcome of my first pregnancy, which left me with a baby intact from circumcision, but not intact in any other way.

Twelve years ago, I went into labor on the morning of New Year's Eve. I went to the hospital, did my breathing, and was so excited and nervous about having my first child. When the doctor came in at 8 a.m., I had been in labor for five hours. He checked me and broke my water. There was meconium in the fluid. We continued with the labor, and by 11 a.m., I was pushing. The labor was progressing, but the baby was also showing signs of distress. Each contraction lowered his heart rate drastically, and it came back up more slowly after each one. We grew more and more anxious, and asked the doctor several times for a cesarean section. Eventually, I did get a cesarean section, as it became an emergency when the baby's heart rate dropped to fifty and did not rebound. When I woke from anesthesia, they told me that my baby had died. His heart beat a few times, but he never took a breath.

A nurse came to see me soon after and asked if I wanted to see the baby. I was horrified. I couldn't imagine why I would want to see any dead baby, never mind my own! But to my surprise, my husband and my mother said yes, they wanted to see Sam. I still refused, so they walked and cried, holding him at the

191

end of my bed. When the nurse came back to take Sam, she said to just let her know if I should change my mind.

My husband told me how beautiful he was, and told me that I should see him. I finally agreed. The nurse gave the baby back to my husband, who laid him on the bed next to me (I couldn't sit up yet because of the cesarean section). I remember him as being so beautiful. He had a perfect head with tiny, wavy curls in his hair. Huge, closed eyes, full lips, my lips, my husband's eyes and ears. He looked like he was sleeping; it was hard to believe he was dead. My husband opened the baby blanket so I could see all of him. He was just cherubic. As I looked at the baby, I felt myself wanting him to stay; I wanted him to be alive, I wanted to take care of him. I didn't want our moment together to end. I asked the nurse to take him back, because I felt myself getting attached, and knew that I couldn't keep him. Looking back, I wish I hadn't cut our moment short. One thing that has stayed with me from that short visit: that baby was perfect. His body was amazing.

Life went on, and I was pregnant again in six months. That did not minimize the amount of pain we felt after losing Sam, and it was an extremely painful year. Even after that first year, moments of great pain and longing have always been present when we think of Sam. When I had my second son, there was no longer any question; I could not circumcise. The thought of putting a knife to something so beautiful and tiny was forever dismissed from my mind. My husband agreed with me.

I also wanted to have the baby sleep with us, so I could keep an eye on him. I was terrified, now, of SIDS. However, I could not sleep with the baby in the bed. He didn't seem to settle down at all, and I was a nervous wreck. If the baby so much as moved his arm, I woke to see what was the matter. And if he didn't move, I woke to make sure he was okay, and still breathing. I kept a tiny mirror next to my bed, and would put it by his little nose and mouth, looking for the fog to confirm that he was still breathing. I moved him across the hall in a month so I could get some sleep.

I have since had three more babies. With my third, a daughter, I was finally able to relax a little. She slept in a bassinet next to my bed, but often we both fell asleep while nursing in bed. My fourth, another son, looked a little like Sam. He also slept next to our bed, but again I often woke to find him next to me in bed. My fifth was totally different. This son would not go to sleep after nursing, unless he was in the bed with us. A very strong-willed little boy, he was also the first to really, *really* want to nurse after a year—a lot.

But by then I knew that babies grow up so fast, and I loved nursing. The experience of losing Sam and my years as a mother gave me the strength to continue to nurse long after his first birthday, regardless of what others thought. I learned that there was a name for the way I was caring for my children: attachment parenting. Although circumcision was the first parenting issue influenced by the loss of our first son, now I see that many of my feelings and decisions as a mother are a result of that first loss. I found other mothers who were also doing AP, and we started a mother's group so we could support each other in the face of a society that seemed to think we were crazy, overindulgent parents. I was amazed at the other mothers who came to practice AP, which is not always easy, without having lost a baby. My devotion to my babies has a lot to do with the baby I couldn't keep. And certainly, the fact that my three living sons are intact has a lot to do with my first perfect baby. And I have often felt, well, not exactly grateful that Sam died, but grateful for the way my life and my living children's lives have changed because I lost Sam.

Donna M. Rucinski Harrington *is the mother of five beautiful children: Sam, Max, Sophie, Luke, and Joe. She lives with her husband and four living children in Massachusetts. She enjoys writing, yoga, and running before the kids wake up, and is embarking on the adventure of homeschooling all four children starting this fall. She participates in a children's writers group, a book club, and AP mother's group, two homeschooling groups, and a knitting group. She often goes to bed early!*

INTACT AND PROUD

Maggie Reilly

My son is intact. In the area of the country I live in, that strikes many people as odd and somewhat surprising. After my son's birth, my husband's aunt asked how my son's circumcision was healing, and upon hearing he was intact, she was shocked. Sadly, she never even thought that it was an option to leave a boy intact. With the exception of my paternal grandfather, no male in either my family or my husband's family has been left intact for generations. My grandfather—the one exception—was always sensitive about his intact state because, in the 1920s, it had been a status symbol to be hospital-born and circumcised.

The only problem with my son being intact is that I feel so strongly about it that I frequently argue for and expound upon the benefits of having an intact son! Most of my family and friends try to avoid the topics of circumcision and breastfeeding with me because I am so adamant about both.

My first memories of circumcision came from a discussion with my mom after reading about circumcision in the biblical story of Abraham. I remember cringing immediately at the thought that someone would take an innocent baby boy and cut part of his penis off. Although I came to the decision much later to leave my son intact, I try to remember the horror I felt at my first initiation to a tradition that was once a biblical one, and now an American one. I would never condemn a circumcision performed out of religious respect, but none of the rest of us should subject our sons to this unfortunate procedure.

Upon becoming pregnant I gave almost no thought to circumcision until I found out I was having a boy. As soon as I learned the news, I immediately knew I wanted to leave him intact. I had been reading everything possible about attachment parenting. Part of respecting my son and his body was leaving him intact. Additionally, I knew from reading that the procedure could leave baby boys in a state of shock and lethargy. My husband, who is circumcised, was initially ambivalent about the decision. As a copious reader, however, I provided him with all of the reputable online sources I had read that had convinced me of the wisdom of leaving our son intact. As soon as he read only a few lines he was highly upset that his parents had—without his consent—removed a natural and healthy part of his body. We immediately agreed that no son of ours would ever undergo the humiliation, pain, and disrespect of a doctor coldly cutting off part of his penis.

The question many people have about our son being intact is what we will tell him if he notices his penis is different from his father's or some of his peers. My husband immediately jumps in and tells people he never noticed anything about his father's penis—except how much bigger it was than his! We both also believe that if our son ever does have questions, we will answer them honestly and give him accurate information about why we believe that no male's penis should be touched without his adult consent.

Neither my husband nor I anticipate any major problems with my son's intact state because of the pride we feel about our decision. Since we are proud of our decision, we hope that our son, too, grows up with a sense of pride and normalcy about his intact penis.

Maggie Reilly *is a mom to a breastfed, intact, and co-sleeping toddler, Benjamin. She enjoys mothering and sewing as well as reading, writing, and discussions about early childhood, parenting, and child advocacy. She, her husband, Josh, and son live in central New Jersey.*

One Mom's Essay on
Making a Decision for Her Child
Jeanne Holden

The day we found out that I was pregnant with my son Cameron was a bitter, cold day in October. The air may have been frigid, but the warmth inside me provided a very comfy home for the precious human being who would be living there. Of course, we didn't know he was a boy at the time. We just knew what a welcome joy he was to our family and to our world.

As any parent would, we became focused, sometimes consumed, with the concept of bringing a child into the world. Doctor's appointments, proper nutrition and exercise, and daily books being read to my belly became second nature. Right from the start my husband, Scott, and I decided what we would and wouldn't accept when it came to the care of our baby. We stood strong and said yes to breastfeeding as long as possible, and no to circumcision right from the start.

Researching is wonderful. I recommend it to anyone who is on the fence or curious about an issue they are interested in learning more about. As first-time parents, my husband and I knew very little about the issues that were presented to us during my pregnancy. We needed to seek help, ask questions, and become informed. This helped us to grow closer and feel good about the decisions we made. The issues became clearer during the researching process, and we were able to discuss them after they were laid out in front of us. We both knew that we wanted nothing to go into our baby, nor did we want our baby to be touched, without our approval.

At the speed of light, four months came around and we were invited to have an ultrasound to see our baby, hear the heartbeat,

197

and find out the sex, if we so desired. We had discussed this decision, and I, being indecisive and pregnant, had mixed feelings.
Ultimately I agreed, and was so excited to hear we were having
a healthy baby boy. My husband looked spaced out, kind of as he
would if he had been offered a seat on the next space shuttle
launch.

Excited? You could say that.

Almost immediately, the research began again. Since we
knew we were having a boy, we focused a lot our attention on
the circumcision issue. We found out that it is performed for
religious reasons, cleanliness reasons, and for general appearance
reasons. Since the religious reasons did not pertain to us, we
were willing to help and show our son how to clean his genitals
properly, and felt appearance had a very low priority, we leaned
toward non-circumcision.

As with anything else, we ultimately needed to make our
own decision. We spoke with parents like us who had sons who
were not circumcised as well as those who were. We went to
websites and read books by parents and doctors alike. An article
in *Men's Health* magazine really got our attention, going into great
detail about the process and how many grown men wish to
reverse it when they are older. For a mainstream magazine, they
really put the facts out there, still leaving their readers to decide
what action to take. Regardless of what others said and did, we
needed to do what we felt was best for our son.

Conversations with my husband brought up wishes on his
part that he was intact, wanting to understand why he had to be
circumcised. Not understanding myself, I expressed my sadness
and had my own feeling of guilt, mainly because as a female I
was never subjected to such an act. Female babies are not altered
in this way, at least not in the hospital I was born in. Infants of
both sexes should be kept as they are, as they were meant to be.
Together, my husband and I stood secure in our belief. Our son
would stay intact and beautiful. No one would remove any part
of him. To us, he was perfect just as he was.

Today, Cameron is five years old and perfectly healthy. He
was breastfed and is not circumcised. Not too long ago he had
some discharge due to the foreskin separation process, and was

given a one hundred percent normal report from his physician. After researching the issue, we found out the correct term for the substance is a "pearl." An e-mail from a sympathetic grandmother, who had the same issue come up with her grandson, reassured it was normal and gave us some insight.

Daily cleansing is very important, and Cameron has learned to take on the job by himself. It will be a lifetime routine, but well worth it. He is very healthy and intact, just the way he was created.

As parents, we need to make our own decisions about our children, born and unborn. Research, talking with others, and having confidence in our opinions is very important. Not feeling alone is such a great feeling. Knowing that there are many others like us who chose to keep their sons intact gives us strength when we become shaky on our journey as caregivers.

Mistakes are made, lessons are learned, and we often kick ourselves over decisions we've made. Following our instincts gave and continues to give my husband and me so much freedom. We can stand proud and walk strong, even if those with whom we walk take a different path.

Jeanne Holden is a stay-at-home mom and writer who resides in Chesapeake, Virginia with her husband, Scott, five-year-old son, Cameron, and two-year-old daughter, Maura. She breastfed both of her children and is very happy with their decision to keep Cameron intact. Her children have inspired her to write children's books.

AN EDUCATED DECISION

Diane Oliver

My first son was born in 1993, in a hospital south of Boston, Massachusetts with the help of a very caring CNM (certified nurse midwife). His birth was an intense, powerful, awesome experience that went flawlessly from start to finish. Several hours after he was born, in the early evening, as my husband and I were basking in the incredible glow of the wonder we had been privileged to parent, someone came into our hospital room and asked us whether or not we planned to circumcise our son. She left some paperwork we had to sign regarding this subject. Now here was a question to which we had not quite come to an answer.

During the pregnancy, we had stopped from time to time to consider whether or not we would circumcise, if we were to have a boy. Each discussion would trail off and end in indecision. My husband, having been born in the late 1950s, was circumcised as a routine procedure, as were my father (to the best of my knowledge!) and my brother. Those were our reference points. I recall that none of this information was particularly helpful at the time.

Later that evening, after my son's birth, my husband and I gathered our wits enough to read through the circumcision paperwork word for word. It explained the procedure, the potential benefits and risks, etc. After we both finished reading the paperwork, we sat on the bed for a few minutes, mulled it over in our own minds for a while, and then looked at each other and said, "Why?" All I can remember now is thinking, "Why would we subject our beautiful, perfect son to this surgical procedure for no reason?" We signed the refused circumcision box

201

right then and there, and that was it for us. The decision was made for this son and any future sons we may be fortunate enough to have.

The next day was an interesting experience for us, and was the beginning of our journey on the "road less traveled" in parenting. Our hospital room was located in a U-shaped end of a corridor. Four of the rooms surrounding us were filled with parents and their newborn baby sons. Five boys, including our son, had been born the day before. It was pretty early in the morning when we heard a nurse outside our room gathering up the baby boys for their circumcisions. We heard her go from room to room saying whether or not the baby would be having the procedure. In a rather cheery voice, we heard her say how this one and this one and this one and this one, all four of the other boys, would be taken for circumcision. When she got to our room, her voice changed to one of slight disapproval and she announced that Baby Boy Oliver would not be getting circumcised. Even in the early morning fog of new parenthood, my husband and I picked up on her tone and realized that we were obviously a thorn in the side of the medical establishment.

Years later, when a good friend of mine was pregnant with her second child, a son, she and I were discussing the issue of circumcision. She and her husband were undecided. She seemed to be leaning toward not circumcising and her husband a bit more toward doing it. Her husband was circumcised, and it appeared to be important to him that his son be "similar." Now there is a reasoning that never did make sense to me or my husband! If Dad has had surgery on some part of his body, then his newborn son should be subjected to an operation so that their body parts look alike? What's up with that? Anyway, this couple did circumcise their son. After they had their son circumcised, they were talking to the dad's mom, and, irony of ironies, she told them that the baby's grandfather had never been circumcised. Is that a kick or what? I am not sure how (or if) they succeeded in rationalizing their decision to circumcise their own son after learning that the baby's father and grandfather were not "similar."

The old saying, "If it ain't broke, don't fix it!" comes to mind when I think of circumcision. Now, ten years after the birth of our first son, we have four boys total, none of whom has needed fixing!

Diane Oliver lives in Wrentham, Massachusetts and is a stay-home-mom to four wonderful boys ages ten, eight, five, and five months. She is an International Board Certified Lactation Consultant in private practice and a La Leche League Leader. Breastfeeding and home birth are near and dear to her heart!

AMBER'S STORY

Amber Craig

When I was eleven years old, I stumbled across an article in *Mothering* magazine about circumcision. At the time, I had no idea what circumcision was—I had never even heard the word before. The article described in agonizing detail how excruciating the circumcision procedure is for the child—it causes pain consistent with torture. I also learned about the possible complications. I remember sitting there with tears in my eyes as I read about strapping a tiny baby to a board and cutting off part of his penis. I absolutely could not imagine why anyone would hurt a little baby. Weren't doctors supposed to be good people? Weren't parents supposed to protect their children from harm? As a naïve child myself, I was disillusioned with society—why would we harm children?

I knew at that moment that I would certainly never allow such a thing to happen to any child I might someday have. I also knew that I had to do everything I could to stop the torture of innocent little boys. By age twelve, I was writing to insurance companies asking them to stop paying for circumcision, and I was handing packets of circumcision information to every pregnant woman I saw.

Fifteen years later, when I was pregnant with my first child, a nurse asked me if I wanted my son circumcised. My first thought was, "The information was out there years ago, surely no one would still be hurting innocent children now that we know better." Unfortunately, I learned this was not the case—many doctors and nurses continued to regularly participate in the torture of baby boys—and at the time of my first son's birth, anesthesia was still pretty rare. Many parents continued to be completely ignorant about circumcision, or were consciously choosing to look the other way while their sons were hurt, just so they could conform to a societal standard.

After the birth of my first son, I became even more committed to doing everything I possibly could to end the involuntary circumcision of innocent children. Once I saw my son, I completely understood that he was born perfect, and I certainly wasn't going to let anyone perform a painful surgery on him. The love for my son grew into a love for all children. Not only did I have an obligation to protect my own son, but I felt a strong obligation to become active in protecting all other babies from genital mutilation.

Three and a half years after the birth of my first son, my second son was born. I now have two beautiful, perfect, intact children. When I first learned about circumcision, I objected to the practice because of the physical pain it caused children. Then I also objected because of the risks it caused babies—bleeding, infection, and in rare cases, even death. Then I learned about the possible sexual losses, both to the male and to his sexual partner—loss of erogenous tissue, loss of lubrication. However, I now get the big picture—it's not the pain or the risks that make circumcision wrong, it's the human rights violations inherent in amputating a normal, healthy body part from a non-consenting minor. The only person who has the right to choose to surgically, cosmetically alter someone's body is that person himself, after reaching adulthood and becoming fully informed. All children, both male and female, have the right to remain genitally intact.

Amber L. Craig *resides in Chapel Hill, North Carolina with her husband and two sons, ages five and two. She is the North Carolina State Director for the National Organization of Circumcision Information Resource Centers.*

IT'S A BOY!

Linda Stallings Gee

The moment the sonographer said, "It's a boy," toward the end of my fourth-month ultrasound, I knew I had a fight ahead of me. Instead of joy and elation, I felt resignation and dread, because I knew my husband and I did not see eye to eye on circumcision. The issue of circumcision first arose when I was pregnant with my first child, who turned out to be a girl. My husband and I hold polar opposite views on the procedure, and after some debating, we chose to curtail the issue until we knew if it was a boy or a girl. When we found out it was a girl, we were both relieved that we wouldn't have to work out the issue that could (jokingly) send us to divorce court.

Over a year and a half later, when we became pregnant with our second child, the subject of circumcision didn't occur to either one of us until the sonographer surprised us with her announcement. I immediately knew the struggle ahead, but it didn't occur to my husband until later, at a celebratory dinner with my parents. Based on his comments at dinner, my stomach sank, and I knew it would taint my feelings of joy about carrying my only son, and indeed it did.

For years before I even considered having children, I deplored the procedure that harmed helpless little boy infants. I felt that it was no less unacceptable and repugnant than the female genital mutilation that takes place in some parts of the world, and which garners antipathy and bewilderment from the "civilized" American world. And yet, a little over half of American parents still choose this elective surgery without much consideration.

For my husband, he was routinely circumcised in the late
'60s. He felt, as do many fathers out there, that his son should
look like him. For me, my son will never look one hundred percent like my husband because of my added genes. In addition,
until my son hits puberty, he won't look like my husband anyway, if at all. They will have bonded in so many wonderful ways
by then that a bit of foreskin would be superfluous in their relationship. In fact, my husband's father wasn't born in America,
and given the traditions of Asia, he was most likely never circumcised either. And that was never an element of their relationship.

Upon doing research and speaking to doctors, we both
found out that circumcision is medically unnecessary. My husband was open to acknowledging that. And in our endeavor to
resolve the issue, we both spoke to many people, some of whom
my husband had known for years without realizing they were
not circumcised. And yet, he was still strongly pushing for a circumcision.

After months of sleepless nights, I finally convinced my husband to see a counselor with me to help us work this all out. In
the session, I explained that it is an irrevocable procedure that we
would be choosing to do for our son, with possible negative side
effects. That as parents wanting the best for our child, why risk
potential harm, especially with a paradigm shift trending towards
people not circumcising their boys anymore? I also told him that
I felt it was selfish for him to want to have a surgical procedure
done on our son so that he and my son could look alike. Would
we ever consider plastic surgery on our newborn daughter so
that her ears would look like mine, or so that her nose would
resemble mine because I was her mommy? Absolutely, unequiv-
ocally not. It would be ludicrous to even entertain the thought
for a second. And yet, in my opinion, that was what my husband
was doing. And deep down, I resented him for that. I resented
him for putting a black cloud over my pregnancy in which I
walked around with a pit in my stomach for months. I just could-
n't understand why this was even an issue!

In our numerous discussions, he would invoke the high
school locker room argument. As a former high school teacher, I
know that very few boys actually undress to bare bottoms in the

locker room, and even fewer actually shower. There's simply not enough time between periods. In addition, it is extremely taboo to look at another's private parts if one should undress all the way. It was really not a valid argument for me.

What I found as the bottom line was that no fact, no argument, no imploration (or bribe!), could appeal to me to change my thinking on circumcision. Being a mother is a huge responsibility, and simple things that I never thought about as an aunt or a babysitter suddenly took on enormous consequences. As a mother, I innately had to protect my child from any unnecessary trauma, even if it was my mate pushing the issue. It boiled down to protecting my son's body. It doesn't belong to me; it doesn't belong to my husband; it belongs to my son. It is a choice that only he can make, and he may choose to have himself circumcised in the future. And in that instance, I will support his choice.

My husband and I never did come to an amicable agreement. I think we both still held out for the miniscule possibility that a girl would actually be birthed on the big day, not a boy. With so much strife between us over the procedure, we stopped discussing it in the end, each hoping the other would capitulate. I, however, just knew I couldn't put my brand new, helpless baby through that. So I simply said no to the nurse when she asked me about his circumcision, and then I told my husband that I would refuse to sign the paperwork in the hospital. I wasn't happy about making such a unilateral decision without his support—we generally tend to get and receive each other's support over big decisions. But in my heart, I knew this was the right choice for my son.

Every time I change his diaper or bathe him, I am so pleased that I didn't allow the circumcision to be done, that I successfully protected him from harm. I feel a rush of warmth toward my son, and an overwhelming surge of love.

I love my husband and I love my son. And my husband loves his son with all his heart. It was a tough road, and there may be bumps in it when my son gets older and curious, but at least I know that I did the best job I could as a mama bear.

Linda Stallings Gee lives in Arizona with her high school sweetheart, her three-year-old daughter, and her eight-month-old son.

TAKING THE WHOLE BABY HOME
Tiffany Palisi

Ask any mother how she would feel if she were told, moments after the birth of her healthy child, that this same child was being taken in for surgery, and she'll tell you that she'd be terrified. Yet thousands of American mothers actually sign a permission sheet giving a doctor the okay—heck, most mothers actually request it—to perform surgery on their newborn babies.

The surgery I am talking about has serious risks and complications that can result in death. Oftentimes, it is performed without any pain medication, forcing the newborn child to go into shock and detach his mind from his body. The baby, who ideally should be alert and suckling at his mother's breast, is out cold—looking to some like a peacefully sleeping baby—in shock from an experience that occurs in his first moments of life.

Following this surgery, the baby suffers through days of agonizing pain without any relief medication. It's a double-edged sword: on the one hand, who wants to pump medication into the pure body of a newborn; on the other hand, what parent wants their child to suffer intense pain when it could be alleviated, at least to some degree, through medication. The answer, clearly, is to say no to the surgery.

Circumcision is a surgery that is elected by a parent for mostly cosmetic reasons, like, "He should look like his dad," or "I want him to look like his peers." Sad, really. Our children will never look just like dad or friends. He will not have the same nose or ears, nor will he have the same body frame. Why should his penis conform to the standards someone else imposed on their child? Because when you think about it, the parent elects this surgery for the child. Can you imagine a parent choosing to give a child a nose job to look more like dad or to prevent the child being heckled in school? It would make major news. But cutting the very important foreskin from the child's penis, his most private body part, is deemed normal. This is not logical.

Why is it not okay for people to perform female genital mutilation but okay to perform male genital mutilation? Many people in our country, America, are fighting to stop female genital mutilation in other countries. Why not fight male genital mutilation—circumcision—here in the United States?

Making the decision not to cut was basically a no-brainer for my husband and me. A man I knew who was in his fifties said, "If you have a boy, don't circumcise him. I'm not circumcised and I've never had a problem with impotence or anything." My response was, "Why would I cut off part of my son's body for no good reason?"

In truth, though, I hadn't thought much about it (being only three months pregnant) so I asked him why he requested this. He said, "I'm just about sixty years old and I've never had a problem with impotence. It's because of my foreskin, you know. That's where all the nerves are. Don't take that away from your son."

I started doing research and found that not only was this man right, but that I could never subject my newborn infant, who'd spent forty weeks in the comfort of my womb, to a painful, unnecessary surgery. Still, I had people telling me I was crazy for many reasons. Here's what they told me and how I responded:

"He'll get made fun of in the locker room."

Well, he probably won't. More and more parents are choosing to keep their boys intact. Plus, the reality is that kids can be made fun of for many reasons. Why not simply give them the tools to deal with teasing and peer pressure? I mentioned this locker room comment to my husband, who laughed and remarked, "Guys just don't look at each other anyway. It's just not cool."

"A circumcised penis is so much cleaner."

The foreskin protects the meatus and glans from urine and feces. It keeps them moist and protects against chafing and other minor injuries. As long as your child is taught good hygiene, as all kids should be, his penis will always be clean. (As a parent, I do nothing to keep the penis clean, just leave it alone.) To clean, the boy should gently slide his foreskin back (when it is retractable, and he'll know when that is), rinse it with warm water, and slide it back in place. Only the boy *himself* should retract his foreskin, and only when *he* is ready).

"Why not circumcise him? It looks so much better."

First, I do not believe a penis looks better or worse when circumcised. Every body is different. As to the question of, "Why not?" the answer is easy. Why subject my healthy son to painful, elective surgery? After seeing a video of circumcision, where the baby is strapped spread eagle to a board and then circumcised without anesthesia or pain medication, I knew I could not do it. Circumcised boys are left with a wound that needs to be kept clean and tended to, and may face further complications like bleeding, infections, urinary retention, and complications from anesthetics (if they are used). Plus, is it really my decision? After all, it's his penis.

"He'll be different than his father."

Yes, he will. His father has brown eyes; his are green-blue. His father has body hair; he has smooth baby skin. He is different than his father in many ways. That's okay. They are each their own unique individuals sharing an amazing relationship with one another. Dads, ask yourself this: is your dad circumcised? I'll bet you either don't know or are incorrect in your assumptions (unless you've already asked).

When the time came to discuss this subject, I approached my husband with caution, as we had not yet talked about it, and he is, in fact, circumcised. I mentioned it to him, and, although he was a bit bothered by the look of an intact penis (I'd shown him medical illustrations to explain the procedure of circumcising), he completely agreed that the surgery was wrong. Barbaric, even. Luckily, I did not have to fight my husband to keep my son intact, as did many of my friends.

. I chose to deliver my baby in a hospital. I was confident that I could protect my baby from being mistakenly circumcised by taking many precautions. First, I made sure that the baby was with either my husband or me at all times, no exceptions. I got advance approval for this arrangement from the maternity wing administrator, informing her that I would go to a local birth center if she would not grant me a non-separation agreement. Then, I clearly stated in my birth plan, which was submitted to both my midwife and the admitting staff at labor and delivery, that my son was not to be circumcised under any circumstances. And finally, I made signs that said, "YES BREASTFEEDING, NO CIR-CUMCISION," to put on the plastic box that the nurses kept in my room, in the event that I wanted to place my precious little baby inside it (and out of my arms? No way!).

I have had quite a difficult time deciding which of my choices was the best for my son. It is between breastfeeding, co-sleeping, and keeping the knife at bay. In the end, I believe that breastfeeding forged a lasting and invaluable bond between us and has kept my son in good health. He is, by the way, still nursing at age two and a half. Additionally, our co-sleeping is amazing. He splits his cuddling time between my husband and me, but when he wakes up in the morning and asks, "Where's Dada, Mama?" and I say, "He's at work, baby," he replies, "Oh. Hold you, Mama," and then gives me a giant hug and kiss followed by, "I love you."

Still, of the three big parenting choices I made, I believe that choosing to keep my son intact was the best decision. His whole penis is his own, not mine. As Brad at NOCIRC (National Organization of Circumcision Information Resource Centers) Texas once put on the bottom of his e-mail, I took "the whole baby home." My husband and I never had to deal with cleaning urine and fecal matter from a bloody wound on our son's penis, nor did we worry about a scab forming or his penis retracting into itself (which often requires that a doctor pull it out from the fatty area that surrounds it). We had none of these troubles because we oppose circumcision, and we gladly allowed our son to keep his whole body, whole.

Tiffany Palisi is the proud mother of John Henry who, at two and a half years old, loves co-sleeping, nursing, and riding in the sling. She functions as a NOCIRC center and loves educating people on natural, attachment parenting.

CO-SLEEPING

"SO, ARE YOU SLEEPING TOGETHER?"
BASIC QUESTIONS FROM A FAMILY PERSPECTIVE
Sylvia Skaggs McTague

Co-sleeping is as much an ethic as a practice. For our family, it started from my husband's and my urge to comfort our baby to sleep rather than ask her to console herself or to conform to a schedule. Although many people do it, it seems like a well-kept secret worth writing about. The timing of my writing is interesting, for my girls just moved to their "own room" a few days ago—but let me save this stage for last, since so many have come before it. For now, I'll just explain: I'm the mother of two. Emma is nearly two and a half, and Tara is nearly one year old. I began motherhood as someone who slept for seven or eight hours almost every night. Since I don't welcome conversations or any complicated interactions at odd hours of the morning, I sought a way that would cause the least disruption to our sleep while still nurturing an infant.

I remember when Emma was a baby and her doctor first announced that we should move her to a crib and let her begin to cry it out in order to adapt her to our lives. Nonchalantly, she explained that unless the baby was crying for a full forty-five minutes before falling asleep, there was really no cause for alarm. I thought, "But after all that crying, how will I go to sleep?" In those days, I had very little detachment from my baby. When Emma cried, I tensed all over, feeling responsible to try to help her. I don't pretend that families who co-sleep somehow avoid crying, but I like it that parents try actively to comfort a baby into sleep, and when at their best, to lull one to sleep before tears occur.

I wonder if the logistics of co-sleep have any effect on a child psychologically. Though I may doze a little myself at the beginning of a baby's nap, most of the time I leave the room after the baby is asleep. So my babies learn to crawl out in the hall or across the living room and find me when they wake up instead of having to call for help from a crib. Recently, during Tara's first nap, I was down in the living room talking to a friend while Emma was playing with one of hers. Suddenly there was a loud rattling from upstairs. "What's that?" my friend gasped. There stood Tara, shaking the gate at the top of the stairs to show that she was ready to join us.

Co-sleeping helps babies articulate themselves better. When a baby cries every time she comes off the breast, even a tired mother realizes that teeth must hurt. I'd hate to lay a baby in a crib in pain, implying that she should just deal with it as if it were any other night.

Co-sleeping has also helped us be more flexible. Currently, Tara may take a first doze while the rest of us are doing anything anywhere. I get some odd looks if she's around my neck while Emma is in a cart at the drugstore or holding my hand at the library; but so be it. One of my fond memories is of Emma falling asleep in a sling while my husband and I walked around the Metropolitan Museum of Art. We try not to let children tie us to the house.

Our family has adapted to so many practices surrounding sleep in such a short period of time: as an infant, Emma usually fell asleep at the breast at about 8:30 p.m. I could be rocking her and singing, catching a rare movie, or even sitting in the living room with friends.

By the time she was around ten months old, we had bought a queen-size bed, for it was too much of a hassle to ease her back into the co-sleeper. About then, she began to crawl out of our bed if I left her—I mean off the bottom, for we had a wall on one side and a bar on the other. It seemed that she'd wake up and seek her parents. After she'd done this twice, I felt like an irresponsible mother, so we moved her to a futon at the foot of our bed. This way at some hour of the morning she'd stand up and whimper to join us where she'd snuggle back to sleep. Once older, my athletic Emma would just climb in by herself.

About three months before Tara arrived, Emma weaned herself from nursing. Getting her to sleep grew harder for a little while, and routine grew more important. I read, rocked, and offered her a bottle to sleep. Though sometimes I'm ready for her to sleep before she is, getting her there helps me relax, and her sense of comfort is priceless.

Generally, I like the way that co-sleeping lets me respond to needs that may differ from night to night. But the week that we brought Tara home, I thought, "Oh no! What have we done?" Emma seemed to buck bedtime altogether and insist on staying with one of her parents till late at night. (I'd been away at the hospital for three nights for the first time since Emma was born, and she had managed well with my husband as well as my mother.) In retrospect, it seems so obvious that late night was finally the time that her sister was not visible, and she was trying to regain security and private time with Mom or Dad. But I was exhausted.

For the next few months, we incorporated that private time into her routine. Emma got a special hour with me at night. We read, talked, and brushed teeth. If Tara voiced a need to join us during that time, my husband would appear and begin to read to Emma while I nursed Tara to sleep. Then, as Robbie disappeared down the stairs with Tara on his shoulder, Emma would say, "Shhh! Baby, Daddy sleeping!" (For a mere five months, Tara often insisted on staying on her father's shoulder. As she grew "older," it was easier for either of us to put her down—in the living room to keep her out of Emma's way.) Keeping everyone peacefully asleep during those months was a pretty intense family commitment.

Since the two sisters have grown more loving and used to one another, they're often together trading parents back and forth till Tara's ready to sleep. Then I nurse and rock Tara to sleep in a separate room, while Robbie and Emma read or do a puzzle. That way, Emma recognizes the order of our last pre-sleep activities. Only sometimes is she too tired to "check and see the moon."

We're lucky that Emma and Tara enjoy time with both parents. My husband and I work as professors in different capacities at a university five minutes from our home. We manage with minimal babysitting. Although Emma may put on a hat, pick up a bag, and proclaim, "I'm going to work!" with self-importance, both girls assume that they're our main focus, and we're always close at hand. I find it kind of funny that they don't recognize any traditional family order or see us as different from themselves—of course, it should be "Baby, Daddy" or "Emma, Mommy" asleep. What else could either parent wish to do?

Soon after Tara's arrival, we decided it was time for Emma to begin sleeping in her own "big girl" bed. We placed it right beside ours because we felt that she wasn't ready to be excluded from the family bed. At some hour of the morning, she'd usually flop at my feet or burrow in with us for warmth and comfort.

Countercultural as it seems, this setup worked for a while. We had one family sleeping room. All other family activities could take place in other rooms. Tara's early snooze in the living room made things a bit more complex, but we're generally quiet people. If something woke Tara up, one of us would just cuddle with her until we were ready to go to sleep ourselves.

Now we've arrived at another stage: three nights ago, Emma and Tara began to share their own room. Emma has her bed, Tara has her futon, and my husband and I have our bed. Having our own bedroom after over two years seems at times romantic and at times kind of strange. The boundaries of that room are still quite fluid. The hall that separates our rooms is about three feet long. I rock or cuddle both girls to sleep separately and then return to any call, sometimes collapsing into Tara's bed or lifting her into my own. These logistics are much more difficult for me for now because I have to get up to provide comfort.

One of my favorite parts of co-sleeping, the morning romps on our bed, still occur when Tara rears up smiling sleepily and when the girls encounter each other. We just all arrive there at different times. Robbie usually takes Tara off for early morning rounds while Emma and I grab a last-hour cuddle and snooze. So far, no one fears sleep. And both girls seem to sense that when they call out, Mom or Dad will respond.

Sylvia Skaggs McTague is the mother of Emma Abigail (two and a half) and Tara Bryn McTague (one). Sylvia grew up in Madison, New Jersey. She left to earn her BA at Bard College and an MA in English at Temple University. She returned to Madison to complete her doctorate at Drew University, where she met her husband, Robert.

After Sylvia and Robert married, they completed their doctorates at Drew, she in English literature and he in history. Currently, they teach at Fairleigh Dickinson University in Madison, where Sylvia is a lecturer. While teaching there, they welcomed both daughters into the world.

Sylvia taught her first college class when she was twenty-one and has been teaching ever since. Now she enjoys as much time as she can, especially long summers off, with her daughters—who learn and grow faster than any other part of her life.

THE COZINESS OF CO-SLEEPING

Sarah J. Buckley

Imagine this. Your baby is two weeks old, and you have finally settled her to sleep for the night in her cot, in the newly painted nursery next to your room. You are awakened from a short but deep sleep by distressed crying, and you stagger out of bed. You turn on the lamp and pick up her up. She is red-faced and too loud for that time of the morning, and her crying has awoken your partner, who you can hear sighing loudly next door.

After a few minutes, you calm her and persuade her to breastfeed. After some time, just as you are about to nod off yourself, she falls off the breast contentedly. Slowly and carefully—you are more awake now, appreciating the delicacy of this maneuver—you slide her into the cot. Only two steps away from the door, and she whimpers. As you turn the door handle, she cries softly, and then increasingly loudly. Your partner, angel that he is, comes in bleary-eyed and offers to walk the corridor with her, which he does for fifteen minutes before putting her gently back in her cot.

"Welcome to parenthood," your friends say, but you can't accept that, or the bone-aching tiredness. Then one day, you discover that you can actually feed her lying down. The next day, as you feel her nestling up against you on the sofa, you begin to wonder if you could feed her like this in bed at night. Your partner is skeptical, and you don't tell anyone else. After a few nights, you realize that if your baby starts the night with you, you don't actually need to get out of bed at all. Your partner is pleased to be hardly disturbed, because you attend to her before she cries, and you feel decidedly brighter in the morning too.

Congratulations. You have rediscovered co-sleeping.

For the millions of years of our human evolution, mothers have slept with their babies; it is what we are adapted for, physiologically, hormonally, and emotionally. The warmth of our bodies, our vigilance even in deep sleep (actually, a breastfeeding, co-sleeping mother spends less time in deep sleep), the easy access to our breast, and the synchronizing of sleep cycles all provide an optimal nighttime environment for our babies.

These benefits are confirmed by the elegant research done by James McKenna, professor of anthropology at University of Notre Dame, Indiana, United States and his colleagues (McKenna, J. and Mosko, S. 1990), who invited thirty-five mother-baby pairs into a sleep research laboratory, and monitored overnight their sleep patterns as they slept together or in separate rooms. They found that not only did co-sleeping pairs get into the same sleep cycles, but that babies who co-slept experienced more frequent "arousals," triggered by the mother's movements, and spent less time in deep sleep.

As a researcher in SIDS, Prof McKenna believes that these low-level arousals, which did not actually awaken either partner, give the baby practice in arousing itself, and may lessen a baby's susceptibility to some forms of SIDS, which are thought to be caused when a baby fails to arouse from deep sleep to reestablish breathing patterns (McKenna, J., Bernshaw, N. 1995).

Professor McKenna speculates that our young are not developmentally prepared to "sleep through" the night in a solitary bed, involving, as this does, long periods of deep sleep (McKenna, J., Bernshaw, N. 1995).

Videos taken during the study showed that co-sleeping mothers, even in deep sleep, seemed   aware of their baby's position, and moved when necessary to avoid overlaying. At no time in the study did co-sleeping mothers impede the breathing of their babies, who had higher average oxygen levels than solitary sleepers.

Although there is no direct evidence to prove Professor McKenna's theories, some of the lowest rates of SIDS are found amongst cultures where co-sleeping is predominant (McKenna, J., Bernshaw, N. 1995).

In fact, on a worldwide basis, co-sleeping is very much the norm (Small, 1998). Even in Western cultures, bed-sharing between mother and nursing baby (usually up to two) was standard practice up until around 150 years ago. Older children would co-sleep with siblings, with a member of the extended family or, for the upper classes, with a servant or nursemaid (Thevenin, 1996).

* * * * *

The 1800s saw the rise of the child-rearing expert—usually male—who emphasized self-reliance from an early age, with strict guidelines for breastfeeding, toilet training, and sleep. Newborns were expected to sleep with their mother, but they were to be removed to an unshared room before the age of one (Thevenin, 1996).

With the Industrial Revolution in the late 1800s, the extended family began to splinter. Mothers became solely responsible for the house and children, and the need for children who required little of her time became paramount. The rise of the germ theory, where the populace was warned not to breathe the air of another, led to a further emphasis on separate sleeping (Thevenin, 1996).

Later in the nineteenth century, smaller and increasingly affluent families began to build houses with separate sleeping quarters so that each child could sleep alone. The myth arose that "cot-death" was caused by mothers overlaying and smothering their babies, which further frightened mothers away from co-sleeping (Thevenin, 1996).

Thankfully, there has been a recent turnaround, and many parents feel more comfortable about sleeping with their babies. Books such as Tine Thevenin's classic, *The Family Bed* (Avery, 1993), have helped to dispel some of the myths around co-sleeping. The most stubborn concern, that of safety, has also been addressed, with recent Western studies showing that co-sleeping does not increase SIDS risk unless co-sleeping parents smoke or use alcohol or drugs (National SIDS Council, 1997).

However, our soft Western bedding may offer more hazards than that of other cultures. Co-sleeping parents need to ensure that their baby's face or head does not become covered by bedding (pillows or quilts can cause problems), that the baby cannot sink into an overly soft mattress—waterbeds are not recommended—and that the baby does not become entrapped, especially in a face-down position (AAP 1997, National SIDS Council, 1997).

Co-sleeping is safe, satisfying and pleasurable; and it's fun to wake up to a cute smile in the mornings. Co-sleeping does not guarantee a full night's sleep—in fact, in McKenna's studies, co-sleeping babies fed more often, (although the mothers usually underestimated this)—but in my experience, waking several times from light sleep is less tiring than the panic and disruption of being woken from deep sleep.

Personally, I have also particularly enjoyed the nighttime intimacy with my second and third babies, for whom daytimes are shared with siblings. Perhaps I have also relaxed, and stopped counting the night wakings, knowing that it passes in its own time and that satisfying my babies' needs is an investment that pays rich dividends.

Sarah J. Buckley is a trained GP (family MD), writer and mother to Emma (thirteen), Zoe (ten), Jacob (eight), and Maia (three), all born ecstatically at home. Her writing on pregnancy, birth, and parenting has been published internationally, and she is currently writing a book about ecstatic birth. She lives in Brisbane, Australia with Nicholas, the love of her life. You can read more of her articles at www.womenofspirit.asn.au/sarahjbuckley.html and you can e-mail her at sarahjbuckley@uqconnect.net.

References

American Academy of Pediatrics. 1997. Does bedsharing affect the risk of SIDS? *Pediatrics* 100(2), 272.

McKenna, J. J., Mosko, S. 1993. Evolution and infant sleep: An experimental study of infant-parent co-sleeping and its implications for SIDS. *Acta Paediatrica Supplement* 389: 31–36.

McKenna, J. J., Bernshaw, N. J. 1995. Breastfeeding and infant-parent co-sleeping as adaptive strategies: are they protective against SIDS? *Breastfeeding: Biocultural Perspectives.*

Stuart-Macadam, P. and Dettwyler, K.A. (eds.) Aldine de Gruyter. 1995. Reducing the risk of Sudden Infant Death Syndrome (SIDS); scientific literature to support the recommendations of the Forum to review the risk factors for SIDS. Convened by the National SIDS Council of Australia, Melbourne, March 1997.

Small, Meredith E. 1998, *Our babies, ourselves.* Doubleday. Quoted in *Mothering* 91 (November/December 1998).

Thevenin, Tine. 1996. The family bed: An age-old concept in child rearing. Avery.

————. In support of the family bed. *Mothering* 84.

Woolridge, M.W. 1995. *Baby-controlled breastfeeding: Biocultural implications.* In Stuart-Macadam and Dettwyler 1995.

✳ ✳ ✳ ✳ ✳

This article was first published in *Nursing Mothers Association of Australia Newsletter*, Vol. 35 No 3, Winter 1999, as "Co-sleeping."

PEACE, WARMTH, AND LOVE
Maggie Reilly

Prior to pregnancy I never really gave much thought to co-sleeping. Upon discovering I was pregnant, I began looking at any and every source of information about child-rearing, focusing especially on breastfeeding. While searching online, I discovered a group of people who practiced attachment parenting. I was immediately fascinated by the principles of attachment and how infants react to the world. After years of studying and teaching in the field of early childhood, I felt that attachment parenting truly embodied the spirit and needs of a child. Everything my husband and I read confirmed our decision to practice attachment parenting. This decision was evident by welcoming our son into the family bed. In fact, we never even purchased a crib—a decision that has raised many guests' eyebrows.

From the hour of my son's birth, he has slept with my husband and me. After he was born, while still in the hospital, he slept on my husband's chest. Upon his arrival home, as he was napping alone, my husband demanded that we lie down with him because he looked so tiny and alone. Even in those first, sleep-deprived weeks, our decision to co-sleep never wavered. Co-sleeping facilitated successful breastfeeding, encouraged bonding, and has made us more responsive parents. Most of the time I can meet my son's nighttime needs without waking by rolling over and offering a sip of breast milk. Even the rough nights resulting from a bout of the croup and teething pains never seemed as bad, since we were all still cuddled snugly in bed. I firmly believe that the strong bond between my husband and son is linked to sharing our sleep together. After a long day with all the stresses of work, my husband is able to come home and meet our son's nighttime needs by being available during his sleep. After all, a nighttime of snuggling is the best reward for a day of stressful meetings and hurried deadlines.

Although my husband and I were at peace with our decision to co-sleep, many others had varying opinions on the matter. We got the occasional whispered confession from people that they too had slept with their babies and enjoyed every minute. All the other comments varied from, "He's going to always want to sleep with you," to "You're starting a bad habit," among other well-known arguments. I have been left with a nagging sense of sorrow for these naysayers. After all, they don't know the joy and pleasure of waking up with a warm, cuddly baby snuggled into them. They have passed up the honor of receiving a dimpled elbow wedged into their ribs. They don't understand the joy of a sleepy, breast-milky laugh first thing in the morning. They have never witnessed the first sunny smile of the day. They have missed the love that comes from meeting a child's nighttime fears. But mostly, they have missed the overwhelming sense of peace that comes from sleeping next to a contented child. Indeed, all is right in the world as we slumber together and share our warmth and love.

Maggie Reilly is a mom to a breastfed, intact, and co-sleeping toddler, Benjamin. She enjoys mothering and sewing, as well as reading, writing, and discussions about early childhood, parenting, and child advocacy. She, her husband, Josh, and son live in Central New Jersey.

TWILIGHT TANGO

Nancy Massotto

Up and over, slide to the left. Roll to the right, then switch sides. Co-sleeping with my nearly-one-year-old son Michael is like a nightly dance. When we are calm and in harmony, our dance is full of gentle motion, restful sleep, and quiet nursing. More often, however, our dance is an awkward combination of tosses and turns, night wakings, and shifting positions.

Sharing my bed with my son wasn't my original intention. In fact, I dutifully purchased both a lovely crib and an Arm's Reach Co-Sleeper (complete with coordinating linens) in eager anticipation of my son's arrival. But Michael immediately demanded otherwise. Those first few weeks he refused to sleep anywhere but on me—nearby simply wasn't good enough. Sleeping side-by-side is thus an improvement for us.

Sure, we tried the co-sleeper. Michael would clench his little fists, pink up his cheeks, and let out a pitiful cry of protest—in spite of the perfectly matching sheets. The clincher came one evening when he was just a few months old. In his deep sleep, I managed to sneak him into the co-sleeper without incident. Just as I was stretching my limbs and reclaiming my bed space, he opened his eyes, reached one hand in my direction and uttered a pleading, "Ma-ma." Thus went the co-sleeper and in came the king-sized bed. And so we dance.

Some mornings I am so exhausted from my evening marathon that I vow to put an end to our tango. I glance longingly at our empty crib, although suspecting that it is much too far away from me. I wonder what it feels like to slumber through the night and to wake up feeling energized. In these trying times I am reassured by a friend, now sleeping four in a bed, who reminds me that before we blink our children will be in high school and sleep will be the least of our concerns. So I stumble through another day happy to have my son by my side.

Soon dusk arrives and my little boy begins to rub his drooping eyes. Our dance begins as we lie down to nurse. A little hand reaches up to twirl my hair. Michael's sucking is rhythmic and his little feet seek out a place to rest up again my thighs. Soon he drifts off—sweet, milky breath filling the air. His hand reaches out, making sure that I am still there, and his entire body relaxes into sleep. I follow his lead into the night, and before I know it, sunlight is peeking through the windows. His huge brown eyes glance over at me and a smile lights up his face. He claps his hands, points to the sky, and begins his morning "dialogue" amid tickles and giggles. I am thankful for our unusually harmonious night. With my entire family within arm's reach, I cannot help but smile at our circumstance. And then I wonder why I would ever consider refusing this dance.

Nancy Massotto is mom to co-sleeping, two-year-old Michael, who was born at home. She is the leader of the Holistic Moms Network, a support group for holistic-minded moms in Northern New Jersey, and is currently a stay-at-home mom. Before starting her family, she was busy completing her PhD in political science.

THE PATH TO SWEET DREAMS
IS NOT PAVED WITH TEARS
Tiffany Palisi

It's tough, sometimes, being a new mother. I am faced with constant questions and as much unwarranted advice. But every single person I meet, even in passing at the grocery store, asks some version of "Is he sleeping through the night yet?" It all seems to begin and end with sleep.

To begin with, sleeping through the night is a relative thing. What constitutes "through the night," when do people expect it to be happening, and why? My Bradley instructor told our class of primiparas that sleeping through the night meant five hours, and that it wouldn't, or shouldn't, happen in the beginning. Nursed babies need to nurse through the night because breast milk metabolizes faster, which causes nurslings to become hungry more frequently. Additionally, night nursing increases the mother's milk supply. Further, babies are needy. They need to eat, drink, and suck, and all with good reason. They aren't being manipulative (they don't know manipulation); they are fighting for survival.

I used to tell people the truth, "No, he's not sleeping through the night yet," and I stopped doing that because the responses were too upsetting. Some said to supplement with formula so my son had a fuller belly, but formula was too great a sacrifice for me. Others suggested giving him cereal at three months. Three months? Even the AAP (whose guidelines are a bit aggressive for me) suggests holding off until six months for a lengthy list of reasons. And finally came the oh-so-popular Ferber method.

The Ferber method, also known as letting baby cry it out, was, as I was told, not even used by Ferber. This fact was printed years ago in a magazine (I was told he reneged publicly in an interview for a New York magazine, probably *The New Yorker*) but no one seems to care. The thing is, when a baby cries, it can mean the baby needs comfort, food, a diaper change, or a change of clothes. It can also mean the baby is scared. When we let a baby cry it out in order to train him to sleep on his own, he receives it as, *I am being left alone in a dark room to cry. My parents cannot hear me or they are not coming to me, so I am not safe. I feel afraid but I am not being rescued. Why aren't they coming?* Eventually, these babies pass out from exhaustion and, after a few nights of this routine, they give up. Some vomit their way through training. Is this healthy?

Clearly, this desire to make our babies independent— what an oxymoron, incidentally, independent babies!—is parent-focused. Our babies take baby steps before they learn to walk, talk, eat, dress, and use the toilet. Yet we are forcing independent sleep on them at far too young an age. How will a child who is Ferberized view sleep? Certainly not as a means of resting or relaxing. I have heard from countless psychiatrists that Ferberized children undergo therapy for major sleep issues during their preteen years. Personally, I think that letting a child cry it out is a cruel manipulation on the part of adults who do not trust their own instincts to meet their babies' needs. I have heard time and again from parents that their pediatrician advised them to let their babies cry it out. Now that's scary.

Regarding sleep, we mothers need to let go. Let go of the clock, the baby trainers—just let go. Letting go is the trick to happiness. And if your baby wants to nurse to sleep, so be it. There is a rumor that nursing a baby to sleep makes their falling to sleep dependent upon having your breast in his or her mouth. It is simply not true. I cannot think of one adult who needs to nurse in order to get to sleep. If your baby needs to rock to sleep, rock her. Again, what adult needs to be held and rocked to sleep at night? Which begs the question, would any decent adult ever let another person cry himself or herself to sleep? All these methods for getting baby to sleep are comfort methods. Comforting our children is part of the maternal job description. We knew that being a caregiver was part of the package before we chose to have our children, now we must step up to the plate and be there for them—give them the care they deserve. Our babies aren't babies forever. One day, your child may have to decide whether to put you in a nursing home or allow you to live with him. Let's teach our kids empathy from the start.

Meeting your child's bedtime needs will affirm, for your child, that sleep is a nice thing. If children are given comfort during childhood, they will enter the world with a good sense of self and will be able to offer themselves comfort. No baby, toddler, or young child should be saddled with this task. The parent's job is to raise the child—not train him.

Sweet dreams.

Tiffany Palisi is the proud mother of John Henry who, at two and a half years old, loves co-sleeping, nursing, and riding in the sling. She functions as a NOCIRC center and loves educating people on natural, attachment parenting.

ON CO-SLEEPING

Jennifer E. Moore

I love sharing a bed. I always have. Even as a child, I would pile up stuffed animals and dolls around me in my bed until I felt so cuddled and warm that I would fall asleep in a heartbeat. I also had a former roommate in college give me the nickname "Thrash," due to my restless sleeping. In the mornings, I would find myself with all the covers and pillows on the floor. My sister and I used to always joke when I was engaged that Andy, my future husband, would need to wear protective gear to bed in order to prevent bruising.

When our son, Sebastian ("Seb"), was born, Andy and I lived in a one-room apartment, (that is one room, not one bedroom!) so as the large majority of new parents do, we set up a crib next to our bed.

I breastfeed, and do so on demand. In the first few weeks after Seb was born, I would get out of bed during the night, and go over to the crib to pick up an already fussy or crying baby to nurse. This went on for about six weeks until Andy attended a new-fathers class at our local hospital. During this class, he learned infant massage, shared the highs and lows of being a new parent with other dads, and also learned about co-sleeping.

After the class, Andy asked me if I wanted to try co-sleeping. I was hesitant, afraid of either rolling over and crushing Seb, or smothering his tiny body in the middle of the night. Since I trust Andy's instincts and ideas, however, I agreed to try it for the night and see how we felt about it in the morning. The night was a normal night in terms of the frequency of Seb's nursing, but I noticed something big: he didn't get to the point of crying at all during the night. Instead, I, almost as in a dream, would offer

239

him my breast before anyone (myself and Andy included) became fully awake and unable to easily fall back asleep. I was amazed! Seb not only didn't cry all night, but I think the three of us actually slept better than when he had been in the crib.

The woman who spoke at Andy's new-fathers class, who is also my lactation consultant, told me later that a mother's body adjusts to having her child nearby in bed, and it is nearly impossible for one to crush a co-sleeping child. This does mean, however, that Andy and I still need to take precautions. No going to bed under the influence of drugs or alcohol, which isn't a problem because I breastfeed, not to mention the kind of environment in which we want to raise our children.

Since Seb sleeps next to me, I am careful about my pillow arrangement, which isn't saying much because I have never really liked pillows under my head at night. I usually use half of one, and the other half is near Andy, who lucks out since he loves pillows and gets all that we have! Our now king-sized bed is placed against our bedroom wall, so Seb has the wall on one side and his momma on the other.

I know some expecting parents who don't even consider co-sleeping, since they like the idea of having their own space at night, and enjoy decorating a nursery. As far as decorating a nursery goes, I don't think a pregnant mother should be exposed to any sort of paint or wallpaper fumes no matter how "harmless" the container claims them to be. I also think that money could be spent on much better things for the new baby, or even for pampering (such as pregnancy massage) for the parents-to-be. Andy and I plan on letting Seb choose the décor for his own room when the time comes, and we don't mind sharing our bed with him. It hasn't hurt our marriage or our sex life, either. Actually, Seb is expecting a new brother or sister in February.

I can't think of a better way for a new baby to feel more welcomed into his or her new family than to be warm and close every night in bed with momma and daddy. In fact, I know a woman and her husband who co-sleep with their three children, ranging in ages from three and a half to newborn. Five people in one bed, and they don't even have a king-sized mattress.

In America, co-sleeping is not "usual" for most families. The reasons vary from the belief that a baby needs to be "independent" from day one (which we don't agree with), to the American dream of every man owning his own piece of property—meaning, for a new baby, having his or her own room and crib. In reference to this point, I have also learned that in previous generations, babies who had their own cribs were usually from wealthier families, and only the poor, "country folk" co-slept. Maybe this stigma still exists in the minds of parents and grandparents. In my opinion, I simply cannot see how placing a baby in a dark room, alone, all night would help a child to sleep better, especially since they may be frightened. Baby monitors will never enter our house. I want to always be close enough to hear my child.

Andy and I still get negative feedback regarding our co-sleeping decision, mostly regarding the belief that Seb won't ever be able to sleep by himself, or that it will be hard to "get him out" when we want him to leave. He just celebrated his first birthday and, trust me, this child can sleep anywhere. Lately, as he gets sleepy, he has started to gravitate towards his own "corner" of our bed and rests his head. Additionally, from what I have been told by other co-sleeping parents, children do not co-sleep forever. Depending on the child, youngsters eventually decide to have their own place to sleep somewhere between two and five years old. In our opinion, Seb is welcome in our bed as long as he desires.

As I mentioned earlier, we are expecting blessing number two in a few months, and both our children will be welcome to continue to sleep with us. Of course, our sleeping arrangement may need to be switched around a little, perhaps the new baby in Seb's old place and him between momma and daddy, but that does not bother us. We used to think that we would try to transition him to his own room—after all, our current apartment has two bedrooms—but after serious consideration, we think, "Why bother." The only reason we would move him would be to satisfy those who ask, "Is he still sleeping in bed with you?" to which our answer will be, for Seb and any other child who desires, "Yes."

Jennifer E. Moore is the mother of one adorable, animal-loving toddler, Sebastian Elihu, and at the time of this article, is expecting child number two in early 2004. Jenn is married to her best friend, Andy, and lives in Central Pennsylvania. She is a stay-at-home mom who also enjoys tie-dying baby clothing. She attends her local La Leche League, MOPS (Mothers of Preschoolers), and in her spare time writes articles for her church newsletter. Jenn and Andy also enjoy discussing attachment parenting with family and friends.

A Special Thank You

Thank you to all of the beautiful, powerful women who are parenting their children in loving, supportive ways. Your experiences are all interwoven with the most basic, natural principles of life. The fact that you have followed your heart and your spirit should make you feel quite proud.

Mothering isn't easy and time is always lacking. I appreciate all the mothers who took a chunk of precious time to visit their computers, probably when they might have been sleeping, to share bits of their adventures as conscious mothers with the rest of the world.

Thank you to Kathy who, for the first two years of my son's life, journeyed with us on the attached path of motherhood, and to my "mom group," including Jen O'Neill, Judy Levinson, Nancy Massotto, Laura Conklin, Tina Mott, Bonnie Lloyd, Ellen Spatola, and Sylvia Skaggs McTague, for always being there and for always supporting my mothering and life choices. I love you all and all of your babies. I've found my tribe.

Johnny, my partner in life and father to our beloved son, thanks for reminding me when I get stressed out that "He's so little." Especially thanks for loving the family bed, for protecting John Henry from circumcision, for helping me learn to breastfeed and change diapers, for being my anchor (physically, emotionally) during the many, many hours of labor, for listening to me complain, and humoring me when I tell you how to parent. John Henry thinks you're the cat's meow, you know, and I do, too.

To my mom, Carolyn M. Klabin, the woman who helps me do everything and loves John Henry like a rock, thank you. You make my day so much brighter (and so much easier). John Henry completely adores you. If the phrase "attached grandmother" were listed in the dictionary, your photo would be printed beside it. God bless you. We love you. And to my daddy, Saul Klabin, without whom I'd be ringing 'em up with the best of them at the corner store. You have given me the opportunity to be a stay-at-home, attached-at-the-hip-and-the-heart-mama. Where do I begin? Lots of love to you.

To G.G. (my Nana) and Papa Nick, and my brother, Justin; thank you for being there as I grew from a child into the woman I am today. Nan, you cleaned my room, played cards with me, let me mess your house up, and, when I was older, went out to dinner with me. We cruised around like two single girls (well, I was) until I met Johnny. Thanks for being my partner in crime. Pop, you drove me to school every morning without fail so that Mommy could stay home and nurse and love little Justin. Our mornings together are ingrained in my memory. Justin, my little big brother, I watched you nurse and co-sleep and saw how happy it made you. Unknowingly, you were my earliest model of an attached child. Thank you. Without every single ounce of life that I lived I would not be who I am today. You all are part of the essence of who I am.

Mumzie, thanks for listening and learning about our parenting choices and for converting into an advocate for breastfeeding, and saying "no" to circumcision. Your grace has been a blessing to our family.

John Henry, blessed angel, spirit baby, beautiful green-eyed love bug, "booty boo," Lord of my heart, you have led me on this journey and continue to do so. You taught me that I couldn't just give up on breastfeeding—you worked really hard at forging that relationship. You were the one who cuddled to me when I placed you on the mattress beside me, who breathed your sweet, sour-dough-smelling breath into my face. You showed me the benefits of the sling when you stopped crying the minute you were in it, or when you hid from strangers beneath the folds of the cloth, or when you fell asleep while I rocked you to Kenny Loggins and later the Gypsy Kings in the comfort of my arms and body. And you give me back, every day, all the love I give you. When I cry and you, at two-and-a-half years old, put your hand on my shoulder, look me in the eyes and ask, "What's wrong? You okay?" petting my shoulder and back all the while, completely one hundred percent sincere, I know that you are the one teaching me. I'm in awe of you.

Printed in the United States
1542200001BB/400-426

9 781587 362774